TERRE HAUTE'S
NOTORIOUS
RED-LIGHT DISTRICT

TERRE HAUTE'S
NOTORIOUS
RED-LIGHT DISTRICT

TIM CRUMRIN

THE
History
PRESS

Published by The History Press
Charleston, SC
www.historypress.com

Front cover, top left: Vigo County Historical Society; *top center*: Vigo County Historical Society; *top right*: Lawson collection; *bottom*: Vigo County Historical Society.
Back cover, left: Lawson collection; *right*: Lawson collection.

First published 2022

Manufactured in the United States

ISBN 9781467151306

Library of Congress Control Number: 2021950607

Notice: The information in this book is true and complete to the best of our knowledge. It is offered without guarantee on the part of the author or The History Press. The author and The History Press disclaim all liability in connection with the use of this book.

Dedicated to Maryln Lawson, who gave this book its heart…

CONTENTS

Acknowledgements   9
Notes on Usage   11
Introduction: The Boundaries of Sin   13

1. The Golden Age   19
2. The Yo-Yo Years: 1918–23   41
3. Settling In: The Second Golden Age and Beyond   47
4. People of the West End   61
5. Madams   79
6. A Girl's Life   87
7. Revival and Decline: 1946–61   99
8. The Long Goodbye: 1962–72   117

Conclusion: Backward Glances   133
Selected Sources   139
About the Author   143

ACKNOWLEDGEMENTS

Historians do not work alone. They have unsung collaborators who aid them in many ways. This book is a prime example. I am indebted to the staff of three local institutions. Sean Eisele of the Special Collections Department at the Vigo County Public Library; Katie Sutrina-Haney and Dennis Vetrovec of the Cunningham Library Special Collections Department at Indiana State University; and Suzy Quick at the Vigo County Historical Society were invaluable to my research. I thank them.

I am also indebted to those who shared their memories of the West End. Cheryl Dean provided her recollections of surveying the Edith Brown house while a member of the Area Planning Commission. Kent Kadel graciously searched the collection of his world-renowned photographer father, Robert Kadel, to provide images for this book. Two anonymous sources offered insightful anecdotes that added to this story. They know who they are, and I thank them. Folksinger/songwriter David Hanners graciously allowed me to include his song about Carl Bauman in the book.

Most of all, I wish to thank Maryln Lawson, who graciously opened her home to me during multiple interviews. Her memories of her parents, Mickey and Maryann Meharry, and the world they lived in helped put the West End in perspective. She, more than anyone, allowed me to try to put all-too-human faces and hearts on those who inhabited the world of the West End. Thank you, Maryln.

NOTES ON USAGE

Throughout this book, I use the words *house* and *girls* as they were employed during the years of the West End. *House* was the most used and the historically correct term for a brothel. I call prostitutes "girls" not as a denigration of women but because that is how they were universally known and how they referred to themselves, no matter their age.

Introduction

THE BOUNDARIES OF SIN

Terre Haute already had a bad reputation by 1906. Newspapers and national magazines called it a "sin city" and a "wide-open town." It was, they said, a lawless town awash with gambling, illegal sales of booze and prostitution. They weren't all wrong.

Under the title "Terre Haute Pictured as a Hell Hole," the *Saturday Spectator* of July 7, 1906, included an editorial sparked by recent out-of-town newspapers' coverage of Terre Haute. The editorial adopted the perpetual "Why is everyone picking on Terre Haute?" response to any negative story on the city.

The article that sparked the outrage had appeared in the *Chicago Tribune*, the most important and widely circulated midwestern paper. It did not hold back: "The red light district is the scene of a hundred all night carousings with the police looking on. The saloons make no pretense of obeying the law. Gambling is lid free. The street and parks are infested with hoodlums who annoy women, and street fights of the most brutal character are common."

The piece is overly dramatic and exaggerated, of course, but is basically correct. Even the *Spectator* editorial did not deny that such conditions existed, only that the allegations were blown out of proportion. There is a very odd assertion in the editorial that the conditions described had existed only during the four years of the administration of Mayor Edwin Bidaman. If the writer truly believed that, he must not have moved to town until 1902.

Terre Haute had a raw edge from its founding in 1816. Perhaps the primary reason for that is simple geography. It was located on the banks of a navigable river, the Wabash. In its second decade, the National Road (the

Terre Haute Pictured as a Hell Hole

Terre Haute is being pictured abroad as a hell hole of vice and municipal corruption, and the situation has reached a point where it demands positive action to clear the blemish in the city's name. The opportunity is at hand by meeting the situation fairly and squarely to go before the world as a reformed town. Metropolitan newspapers ordinarily reliable have shown up bad things in Terre Haute without mentioning the good. The purpose is to make Terre Haute an example of what is happening in the cities where the newspapers containing the lurid reports are printed. Conditions there are not better, but powerful as the papers are they dare not present the truth about men and conditions in towns where they are published. A town many miles distant is pounced upon to show what effect evils unchecked have on a community. The purpose is to warn their own people and frighten politicians by holding up as a terrible example conditions in a distant town. The report has gone out Terre Haute has impeached its mayor because he would not enforce laws and that the town is so brazen the bartenders' union had no hesitancy in openly declaring a boycott against members of a council who wanted better things. Away from Terre Haute this appears to be a brazen effrontery, disclosing a rotten condition, else the bartenders would not dare to order a boycott because some men sought to do their duty in removing a mayor who failed to enforced liquor laws. In the outside newspaper accounts it is said the distillery and brewery interests have held absolute power. People away from here reading the metropolitan papers know of no extenuating circumstances, and they believe in Terre Haute a man who tries to enforce law is to be boycotted. Editorials are being written on this bold action from coast to coast. At home we know we have a town better than a majority of cities. The conditions in other cities are not exposed. But Terre Haute has never lived down its reputation made during the former administration when murders were weekly occurrences in saloons, gambling was permitted on the streets, robberies and hold-ups in the west end were reported nightly, and vice was to be found on every hand. Traveling men spread these reports, verifying and enlarging on what was printed by foreign papers. The improvement in the last two years has not been heralded abroad. It will take twenty years to live down the reputation established in four years unless drastic steps are taken at once—sensational enough to create an outside ripple and make the newspapers play Terre Haute up as a reform city. This seems to be the only alternative since the city stands before the world as one to be pointed out as an awful example. The Chicago Tribune, having the reputation of being a conservative paper, devoted three columns yesterday to a most lurid account of conditions in Terre Haute. Extracts are reprinted not because they are endorsed, but to show what is being put before the public in papers of immense circulation, influence and with reputations for being reliable. It is to be noticed reference is not confined to the mayoralty controversy.

Both sides in the mayoralty fight, which is disrupting the city and had led to a state of anarchy, today took action in the courts in an effort to gain the upper hand.

• • •

With the municipal situation growing out of the impeachment of Mayor Edwin J. Bidaman tangled into a sailor's knot by injunctions and court orders the rudderless ship of state is sailing on an open sea of vice. The deposed mayor, determined to conquer or crush, is like a bull in a china shop, and public business is at a standstill. Riot talk is in the air, for the city is evenly divided in the struggle, and no proceedings pending in the courts can decide the title of Mayor. The last two meetings of the common council have been attended by threats and armed forces and disorderly adjournments. To cap the climax the bar-

cilmen who voted against a wide open town.

The situation is dramatic in the extreme. It is the life and death struggle for control of the council between the new party shouting under the banner of reform and the old "vested interests" which have been accustomed to dictate municipal affairs for twenty years.

The city is reveling in the laxity of administration. The red light district is the scene of a hundred all night carousals with the police looking on. The saloons make no pretense of obeying the law. Gambling is lid free. The streets and parks are infested with drunken hoodlums who annoy women, and street fights of the most brutal character are common.

It is a modern Jericho, only to be cleansed by burning, according to the Rev. Charles William Tinsley, pastor of the leading church of the city, who is about to forsake the city because he fears his once breathe an atmosphere so tainted with vice, infidelity and low civic ideals.

This municipal muddle is the anticlimax to the great fight which the Manufacturers' club and minor reform organizations started for pure city government last winter. That fight failed, and the aroused people sunk back into their old apathy under the domination of the saloons, the gamblers, and the financial and political "bosses." Now no one is sure whether he is facing the square issue of reform and graft or whether the new movement is not a deeper issue with the same false and in view. The pendulum of public opinion is swinging with every new wind.

• • •

Terre Haute is a fair city in its physical aspects. Its public buildings are imposing, its streets wide and clean, its residences showing widely distributed wealth. Great breweries and factories overshadow the city and provide work for 40,000 laborers. There are good school houses, a state Normal school, and several church spires rising out of the shady streets.

It is still a provincial town. The people still call the principal business street "Main street," although it is named Wabash avenue. There is a pushing, hustling atmosphere in the business section and men are pointed out as millionaires who wear cheap clothes and eat in cheap restaurants. But it is in morals, both public and private, that the city fails to live up to the average municipality. Built out of the population of Old Vincennes, the stronghold of French infidelity, the attempt to graft Puritanical ideals has resulted in confusion. The passion for municipal reform and "trust busting" which has swept down the ancient political barriers in the great cities of the country has precolated in diluted drops to this southern Indiana community.

• • •

Last week, with but two months more to serve, the second impeachment was brought. Kehoe denied that he had anything to do with it, the Manufacturers' club will not admit it, and it rests with the majority members of the council whose motive is said by Bidaman to be a political game.

Four councilmen obtained the evidence. They made a trip to the slums and found policemen dancing on the street with women and entering disorderly houses to take part in the ribaldry, not to stop it. They found women on the streets who accosted them. They found saloons open all night and liquor being sold in places without a license. Then they told of these things and voted by a count of six to three to remove the mayor.

• • •

"Everything has been legal in the ousting of Bidaman," said President Reading of the Manufacturers' club. "The council acted as the United States senate would do.

"Bidaman failed to keep his pledges and he wilfully allowed the laws to be broken. Backingham is mayor. He will remain so until September. He will keep the control of the purse, and that is the important thing. He will throw out every policeman who sticks to Bid-

Saturday Spectator article, 1906. *Author collection.*

country's first interstate) sliced through the middle of town. The city became a major railroad junction, with both north–south and east–west rail lines going through town. During the brief canal era in Indiana, the city was part of the Wabash and Erie Canal system.

Thus Terre Haute was a transportation hub with a huge number of transients, mostly male. At any one time, there were boatmen, construction workers, railroaders and travelers teeming through the city. When you have a town filled with lonely men thirsty for a drink and hungry for a woman, there are people more than eager to sate their desires—for a price. Brothels, gambling dens and wild saloons were always present and served as drivers of the city's economy.

The *Tribune* article contributed to the renewed efforts to "regulate" the West End once more. A key phrase in the article was "streets and parks." There were brothels in all areas of Terre Haute, even the "upscale" neighborhoods. It is likely that someone was within an easy walk to a brothel, no matter what part of the city. Of course, that angered the good citizens. They constantly made complaints to officials. "Get them out of my backyard" was the cry.

There had been earlier efforts to set boundaries, but in the Terre Haute tradition, enforcement was lax. Things came to a head in the summer of 1906. Bidaman was impeached in July due to his hands-off policy on vice. There was impetus for change. On August 6, the Common Council accepted the recommendation of the Board of Public Safety to set boundaries for the West End. Originally, the council wanted to end the eastern border at Third Street, but it kept creeping to Fourth Street. The de facto borders became the Wabash River on the west to Fourth Street; Cherry Street was the southern boundary, Eagle Street the northern. The West End's borders were basically set for the next sixty-five years.

It may seem odd to some that a city would "officially recognize" vice and accept its presence, but Terre Haute was actually following a national trend that began in the 1890s. The more advanced and far-thinking reformers, sometimes known as "mugwumps," felt that "reputational segregation" of vices like gambling, prostitution and saloons into a designated area benefited the city and its population. They believed a segregated area would weaken working-class political parties by restricting the areas where candidates could meet voters and have a ready source of income from payoffs by vice operators. By concentrating these parties into one tiny part of town, it would weaken their chances to control citywide elections. As we shall see, the reformers' expectations did not reckon with West End and Terre Haute politics.

Thus, Terre Haute was following in the footsteps of cities like New Orleans, Shreveport and Houston. There were outcries that by creating red-light districts through official ordinances, cities were condoning and legalizing vice. It was unconstitutional, they cried. Not so, said the U.S. Supreme Court in 1900. Cities were merely using "legitimately exercised local police powers."

WHY THE WEST END

Why was this particular area chosen to be the "official" red-light district? First and most importantly, it was already there. Brothels and saloons had littered the waterfront area since the Civil War. There were likely over twenty-five brothels within the borders already. The 1900 census offered ample evidence of this. In just two blocks, seventy-nine women identified themselves as either keeper of a house of ill fame or "sporting." *Sporting* was a period term for prostitute.

The West End between the river and Second Street was not one of the most desirable areas in Terre Haute. It was never a planned area. People just threw up shacks and tents. It was directly across the river from the town dump and crematorium. In all but the coldest weather, a miasma of smells settled over the area. It was the site of longtime pork-processing plants. Living there was rather like living across from the Chicago stockyards on a smaller scale. It was nestled between the Wabash River Bridge and the railroad trestle, so there was constant traffic and noise.

But the eastern half of the district had once been a desirable area with nice homes. In the 1880s, it was home to a few of the city's better families. In the two decades before the regulation, that part of the West End was filled with residences, small business firms and grocery stores. It also had a sizable number of boardinghouses, duplexes and up and downers—two-story multiple-occupancy houses. These were easily turned into the larger brothels.

The people already living there would have no say in the decision. The vast majority of residents were renters. Their houses were owned by developers, city officials and other absentee landlords. Who would give a damn about what these residents thought? They were already living near an area of seedy saloons, gambling dens and brothels. They were used to disease, poverty and violence. Just look at those people in Jockey Alley, for god sakes!

Jockey Alley was a squalid area a half block north of the courthouse between First and Second Streets. It was long known as a place of "broken-down horses, derelicts and the riff raff of humanity." It got its name because it was the place horse traders gathered in the nineteenth century. It became a place of hovels, raw sewage and the residence of last resort of Terre Haute's poorest of the poor. The people there were called the "drifting class, those without family or other ties, no future, and usually a past devoid of anything except poverty, filth and degeneracy." The only horse trading still done was the raffling of broken-down horses to local ragpickers, who used them until they died and returned looking for a replacement.

The "residents" lived in a series of rickety sheds with one window and a door that opened into the filthy alley. It was often a place of violence arising from domestic quarrels, saloon fights and grudges long and shortly held.

Ironically, the council's "redistricting" of the West End began something of an urban renewal project for the area. With brothels relocating to the West End, a building boomlet started. Old structures were demolished and much nicer housing went up. Much of the land and new houses were owned by some Terre Haute movers and shakers, including politicians like future mayor Donn Roberts. As always, they saw a chance for a quick profit.

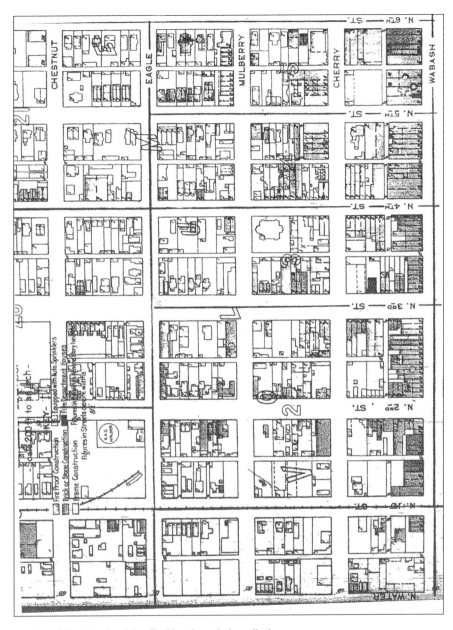

Sanborn Map showing West End borders. *Author collection.*

Police made it known to those maintaining houses outside of the West End that they were facing increased scrutiny. They might want to consider a move to the red-light district. As further incentive to move, a few more arrests were made. Saloons that hosted streetwalkers were more liable to raids. Word soon got around that the West End was the place to be if you wanted to operate relatively unmolested—if you kept your nose clean.

Some may wonder why the city allowed the red-light district to be located literally across the street from the courthouse and a block from the county jail. In theory, this allowed authorities to keep a close eye on the goings-on. If things got out hand, they were there to tamp it back down. In many ways, that was the case. Cynics might say it allowed officials to keep an eye on a source of their tainted income.

Underlying all of this were some basic home truths. There will always be vice. It has always been with us. You cannot successfully legislate morality in all cases. The borders were meant to contain vice in a discrete area and keep it from seeping into the wider community.

In her book *Lost Sisterhood*, Ruth Rosen includes a quote from sociologist Jennifer James on prostitution that aptly describes the next six decades in Terre Haute. "Authorities…found themselves making moral laws to satisfy one group, then not enforcing these laws to satisfy one group and, finally, selectively enforcing the laws to satisfy a third group."

1

THE GOLDEN AGE

There are differing theories as to what years comprised the "Golden Age" of the West End. Some believe it lasted only from 1906 to 1917. Others think it extended until the coming of World War II. However, a closer examination suggests that there were two phases of the golden age. The first from 1906 to 1917, the second from 1923 until Prohibition ended in 1933.

THE WILD YEARS: 1906–17

With official borders in place and more and more houses sprouting up, the West End awoke in the new year of 1907 with a massive and collective hangover. In the relatively quiet hours after dawn, some must have realized that from now on, every night would be New Year's Eve in the West End. Open nearly every hour of the day of every week, the district had on offer what many wanted: women, whiskey and enticing games of chance.

In those early years, the West End truly resembled a rootin', tootin' Wild West town more than a midwestern neighborhood. The streets were mostly unpaved. Horses were everywhere. Ruel Burns, who loved delivering telegrams to the area because the madams were generous tippers, likened it to a small village. There were seemingly saloons on every corner—and some in between. *Saloons* is the correct term. These were not bars or taverns or genteel lounges in swanky hotels. These were mainly rough-hewn places with dirt floors or rough wooden ones covered with sawdust and spittoons. Their customers were not doctors, lawyers or businessmen but workingmen and, occasionally, women. They hosted brawls, not scuffles. Many of the fights spilled onto the streets, where they joined a cacophony of boisterous noise and loud music. The West End was not a sedate place.

On many long nights, visitors heard the West End for several blocks before they set foot inside its borders. Music blared from saloons. Alcohol-infused revelers shared their singing talents at full volume as they stumbled through the streets. Gunshots cracked through the air and, sometimes, through the bodies of victims. Girls in skimpy costumes from some of the houses would shout out to potential customers from windows or porches. If that failed, many took to the uproar in the streets to grab men and offer their services. If that failed, a costume malfunction occurred, revealing what the men might be missing. If some men were still not convinced, a well-placed prostitute's hand might seal the deal.

Men roamed up and down the streets, going from bar to bar or from bar to brothel and back again. Nothing topped off a visit to a prostitute like heading to a saloon for a smoke and a drink. A person could then maybe try their hand at a game of chance in the back room. The West End was a one-stop pleasure dome. The streets also had their full share of muggers, pickpockets and thieves. One editorial noted that there were so many holdup men in the West End that "no man with a five dollar bill" had a ghost of a chance of not being slugged and robbed.

Saloons were also scenes of thefts, both petty and large. Ed Light's saloon on North Third Street was a place where wallets left lighter than when they entered, and not just from buying booze. Pickpockets found it was much easier to relieve the wallet or jewelry from a man who had bent his elbow a few times too many. If stealth wasn't one's preferred means of committing robbery, there were more direct methods. A Clinton, Indiana man named John Dorito made the mistake of taking his thirst to Light's saloon in 1918. A dazed Dorito later stumbled his way into the police station to report that he had been drugged and robbed of fifteen dollars and his pocket watch by a woman in the saloon. Being "slipped a mickey" was a time-honored tradition in some West End saloons.

The king of the West End was Frank "Buster" Clark. Buster was a big man in more ways than one. Over six feet tall and carrying over 250 pounds, Buster was a man for all seasons. Pimp, drug dealer, bootlegger,

Interior of Ed Light's saloon in the West End. *Vigo County Historical Society.*

thief, saloon owner, gambler, political fixer, fence, thug, tax cheat—Buster did it all. Little went on in the West End without Buster's knowledge or approval. He was known for his "absolute reign" over the district. Among his powers was the ability to have any police officer doing his job too zealously removed and reassigned. When an officer named Jones had the affrontery to make madams and saloonkeepers follow regulations, he was quickly removed. Among his sins was keeping an eye out for drunks who were easy prey for a quick mugging. Jones would arrest the man to keep him out of harm's way or find his buddies to take him home.

Gambling and alcohol fueled the vast majority of violence in the West End. They were a volatile combination. If a man spent his earnings in a brothel, he considered it money well spent. He got what he wanted. If he anted up that same amount of money in a saloon card game and felt he was cheated, he looked for revenge. Two of the worst incidents involved Black gambling den operators Pleasant Cooksey and George "Honey Boy" Evans. Both were accused of dealing from the bottom of the deck by aggrieved card players. Evans's antagonist drew a sharp knife from his boot and nearly beheaded him, while Cooksey was shot in the back during a street fair.

And there were many saloons and a lot of gambling in the district. It would be nearly impossible to find a saloon that didn't have card games, roulette wheels or a slot machine in the back room or upstairs. One source suggested that there were five gamblers for every prostitute in the West End.

One of the more innovative gambling scams was practiced by Luke Fogel and John Dobbs on the second floor of their saloon, the Hinky Dink. They used a shill called a "plugger" to draw the gullible into the game. Typically, the plugger would pose as a well-dressed man hanging about local hotels, most often the swanky Terre Haute House. He would strike up a conversation with the mark. He would say Terre Haute is the "widest-open town in the United States. I'm a stranger here, but I've traveled from coast to coast and have seen gambling at its best. But this town has them all beat."

Naturally intrigued, the man would ask what he meant. The plugger would say that he saw a game at the Hinky Dink that was a "square game"— an honest-to-god fair game. The hook was set, and the man would head on down to the Hinky Dink to try his luck at the "green cloth game."

He would stand before a table with a green cloth with numbers painted on it. It was explained to him that two or three of the numbers were "house numbers." If the spinning spindle stopped on one of those, the house won the bet. If it landed on any other number, the player won. The mark would squeeze the spindle and naturally won the bet right away. Of course, he won several games and wanted to continue. Then he was told that if he landed on a "jackpot" square he must double the bet or lose. The "house" then had the right to double his bet. So the player's original two-dollar bet was now upped to eight dollars. After that, miracle of miracles, the spindle stops only on the jackpot squares. Eventually, the sucker runs out of money, loses the game and goes home broke while Fogel and Dobbs count the winnings. Another lesson (hopefully) learned in the West End.

The pair were eventually arrested and sued by the wife of one of the losers, but the case never went to trial.

By 1911, the West End had grown. There were an estimated fifty-plus brothels. This number did not include the girls working the saloons and gambling dens, which often set aside rooms for prostitutes to host their clients. In addition, there were hotels on the fringes of the district and private houses where rooms could be rented to conduct business. Coming up with actual numbers for brothels and prostitutes is a near impossible task. They were either overestimated or undercounted, depending on who was offering up figures. Reformers were always erring on the high side to make their point, while politicians and police thought it best to go low to save face during calls to clamp down on the district.

One historian gave a wildly exaggerated number of 3,500 working prostitutes in the district during the golden ages. With the use of census data, city directories and arrest records, the figures are probably closer to sixty brothels and up to 900 full- and part-time prostitutes working in the district at its zenith. This does not count those working outside of the West End in smaller brothels and apartments or working as bar girls. That number was probably 150 to 200 working girls.

There was always a hierarchy among the houses in the West End. The more upscale brothels tended to cluster around North Second Street, while the others operated more on the fringes of the district. This was especially true of Black brothels, which were always looked down on. They were mainly located around the outer limits of the West End on Water Street and North Third and Fourth Streets. Black houses were always considered the most rowdy and raucous and their girls the most outrageous in efforts to attract customers. For those reasons, and due to simple prejudice, Black houses were raided more often than were White brothels.

The West End was both integrated and segregated. Black brothels were occasionally located next door to White brothels, but they were mostly separate worlds. White men were eagerly accepted at Black houses, but the reverse was certainly not true. Despite what some people think, Black men being admitted to White houses rarely, if ever, occurred. A later madam in an upscale White brothel recalled the temerity of a Black man trying to enter. He was intercepted by the Black maid at the door, who told him to "get his Black ass away from here and go where you belong." Similarly, there seems to be no record of a Black girl working in a White house.

Black madams and girls were singled out for some of the most scurrilous attacks by the press and police. Madam Lulu Brown, who had been running brothels since the 1880s, was described as a "negro wench of infamous reputation." Her house was condemned as a "Foul Dive" and she and her girls as a "leprous family" of whores "with characters much darker than their black skin."

The West End reflected other red-light districts around the nation in that it was a multiracial community. Generally, the racial makeup of districts reflected the general population, and that appears to be the case in the West End. One thing is certain: Black brothels were at the bottom of the caste system.

But all levels of madams and houses paled in comparison to one woman and her house. And she would reign over the West End for forty years.

QUEEN OF THE WEST END

Some just have a regal aura about them, even if they were not to the manor born. Edith Brown was one of those people. She was born in 1878 on a hardscrabble farm outside Paris, Illinois, to George and Emaline Brown. It was not the sort of place likely to hold a young girl with drive and ambition. Luckily, her father, tired of being a lowly farm laborer, moved the family to Terre Haute in 1891. He found a job as a carpenter at a pianoforte box maker.

By 1896, the teenage Edith was working as a live-in domestic servant in the home of prominent furniture store owner John Dobbs. But working as a maid for three dollars a week was not what Edith had in mind for herself. Miss Edith Brown, as she listed herself in the city director, was looking for something better. Soon, likely through Dobbs, she caught the eye of another furniture dealer in town. Edith had her sugar daddy, a man whose money would finance her ambition. Three years later, she was Madam Edith Brown.

Why did a bright, attractive woman with a head for business choose the world's oldest profession as her own? We will never know for certain. Edith could be very enigmatic. Perhaps being so bright, she realized that in the world she lived in, it was one of the best ways for a single woman to control her own destiny and fortunes.

She hired her "staff" and set up business at first at a "house" at 211 North First in 1899. When the 1900 census worker came, she told him she

Edith Brown, circa 1915. *Vigo County Historical Society.*

was single and the head of the house and gave her profession as "sporting." She was twenty years old and had two other young women living in the house: Catherine, twenty-one, and Jennie, eighteen.

Around 1901, she moved to a larger, two-story brick house at 213 Mulberry. Her business grew steadily. Word got around that there was something about Edith Brown's place and her girls. Brown was always looking to improve her situation, and she moved to an even nicer house at 318 Eagle in 1906. Each move was a step up. Each house was better than the previous one. Each new house was fancier than all others in the West End.

Edith Brown's third house, circa 1913. *Vigo County Historical Society*.

Edith Brown's "staff," circa 1915.
Vigo County Historical Society.

THE MONK

It was one of those sweat-dripping August nights in 1914. Around a table in McGinty's Saloon, four men, including Deputy Sheriff Feller and saloon owner John Hutchinson, sat playing poker when Flossie Irwin walked in. Flossie, the madam of a house on North Second, came in looking to exchange a fifty-cent piece for nickels. She sought out the owner's wife and, looking frightened, reportedly told her that Monk Burke was looking for her. And that he was carrying a gun. Mrs. Hutchinson told Flossie to go find the police officer patrolling the district.

Just then, Burke walked in with two of his cronies, Webb Berry and Carl Scott. Monk was "crazed with liquor and cocaine." Spotting Flossie, he demanded she give him two dollars for drinks. When she refused, he shambled over to the poker players and borrowed the money from them. After buying the drinks, he headed for the door but paused as if thinking something over.

He stumbled over and stood behind Irwin. She stiffened and told him not to pull the gun. Burked just stared at her—a hard, bitter glare. "You were nothing but a no account ——," he told her. He lifted the gun and shot her in the head. When Flossie fell to the barroom floor, he shot her twice more. Seemingly calm, Burke walked out the side door. The deputy went after him. As he started to question him, Burke raised the gun with both hands and shot himself in the temple. He was soon dead.

The morgue attendants were called to carry the bodies out of the West End. Flossie was Burke's ex-wife. Strangely, another of her ex-husbands had been killed in a gun battle the previous year. Flossie Irwin was a woman who just could not escape death.

Only later was it learned that Burke did not set out to kill her that night.

Some believed the "System" was the cause of Flossie Irwin's murder. The System was the political machine that protected and controlled much of the vice in Terre Haute. It used whatever means necessary, whether "mailed fist or protective hand," to ensure its control over the West End or other territories within its realm. Poor Flossie was the unwitting victim of a "business" dispute between two West End saloonkeepers.

Jack Hines, ace fixer and political string-puller, ran a West End saloon on land owned by Donn Roberts. Sometime prostitute Bessie Moore "worked" in the restaurant in the back. She was a "booster" who brought in a lot of business from the hungry men in the district. Bessie's lover was Wes Godfrey, a West End all-arounder whose regular haunt was Jack

Tierney's saloon on Wabash Avenue. It just didn't seem right to Wes that his girl, a "known drawing card," was not pulling the boys in to his buddy Tierney's saloon. He persuaded her to move to Hinky Dink to ply her successful trade there.

That did not sit well with Jack Hines. He hustled over to see Assistant Chief of Police Jack Nugent to plead his case. Nugent was known to go all shaky in the knees at the mention of Hine's name and wasted no time in making his decision. To carry out the directive, he turned to Monk Burke. Monk was well known as a fellow who could use his influence to make wrongs right again. His reputation in the West End was of a man who "could smooth the tangles out of almost any situation."

Nugent told him that Bessie had better return to Hines or she would face banishment from the West End. Burke set about to work his magic. He called Bessie to the police station, where she was given the ultimatum: go to Hines or go home.

An upset Bessie went immediately to tell Godfrey the verdict. Godfrey's well-known temper erupted immediately. He told her not to worry. Before that happened, he would "furnish business for the undertaker." He was going to get Monk Burke.

Word moved fleetly through the West End. In no time, Burke heard about the threat. He decided to strike first. It would be like a scene from the Old West: two gunfighters stalking each other through the dusty streets. After filling himself with whiskey and cocaine and his revolver with bullets, Burke went in search of Godfrey. He tried Tierney's saloon first. With no Wes Godfrey in sight, he set out to search for him in various saloons. His next stop was McGinty's.

In many ways, Jack Nugent was the poster boy for the policemen enmeshed in the political corruption that was a daily part of the West End. He moved up the ladder by doing whatever he was told to do. If a guilty party with pull was brought to jail, he arranged for them to be unguilty. If a West End character was not doing as told, Nugent would make trouble for them. A madam could suddenly find herself or her girls arrested. A saloonkeeper could find his place closed down. It didn't pay to buck the System.

Variations of the System existed throughout the life of the West End. But its worst version occurred during the administration of Donn Roberts. Donn M. Roberts was the most corrupt politician in Terre Haute history— no mean feat in itself. The son of a well-regarded physician, Donn was a clever lad. He graduated from Rose Polytechnic and later trained as a lawyer. He ran a construction company and learned about political wheeling and dealing while finagling city contracts for roads and sewers. He was appointed city engineer in 1910 but was fired the next year after disagreements with the mayor he had supported. That was not going to stop Donn Roberts's political ambitions.

WHO'S PULLING THE STRINGS?

The West End could be both the puppet and the puppeteer, depending on the circumstances. This was particularly true during Terre Haute's noticeably corrupt election cycles. Politicians knew that the West End was vital to winning citywide races. Most of the time, corruption involved vote buying. A man's vote could be bought for a dollar and a token for a free beer at West End saloons. Money was also paid to those who voted early and often. Ballot boxes within the precincts could mysteriously disappear or contain more ballots than eligible voters. The actual buying of votes was mainly left to saloonkeepers or other administration apparatchiks, like Buster Clark or Jack Hines, who were the usual go-betweens on any issue.

But in 1913, Donn Roberts decided to go all-out to steal the election, with help from the West End. When "Duh Mayor" schemed, he schemed big.

Roberts's plan was audacious but simple. He would swell the voter rolls with 2,500 false registrants. In the November election, even the dead would be voting for Donn Roberts. He set his minions to work, enlisting West End saloonkeepers. hangers-on and cronies like Jack Hines, Jack Nugent and Buster Clark. It must have been tough for Buster, who was a Republican and no fan of the renegade Democrat Roberts, who was not even supported by the regular Democratic organization.

They set to work. Suddenly, hundreds of "voters" were registered at the addresses of schools, vacant lots, storefronts and—surprise!—saloons. Two hundred voters listed their home address as Frank Hess's Midway saloon. Two other bars were suddenly "home" to sixty and one hundred others. Nearly every saloon now had tenants. It was not limited to the West End. Crawford Fairbanks, owner of the Terre Haute Brewing Company, was a big Roberts supporter and was rumored to own or control over 150 bars in the city. That helped, but the key as always was the red-light district.

Once the registration card scheme was completed, it was time to move on to phase two of the plan. A huge slush fund was created to buy the votes of genuine voters and pay all the "repeaters" who would be needed to assume different names and vote early and very often. The money would be distributed by bartenders and Roberts henchmen. Not one to leave anything to chance, Roberts enlisted the president of the Board of Works and mechanical wizard Harry Montgomery to rig the supposedly tamper-proof voting machines recently purchased by the city.

All was ready for the November election. The Roberts bullies were in place to intimidate election watchers and voters. Bartenders stood ready to pay the repeaters. Buster Clark bought six hundred votes for a dollar each. The going rate was a dollar, but some got five dollars per vote, though especially swift and reliable repeaters might get as much as eight dollars. Saloonkeepers, certain that a good deal of that money would flow back into their places, were happy to help the cause. Voters were herded to the polls. Even legitimate voters got a little something for casting their ballot for Donn: a token for a free beer at their favorite elbow bender.

There were other little tricks, like arresting the official poll watchers and election officials and holding them without bail until the polls closed, or planting guns on known Republican voters and reporting them to the police for violating laws against firearms in polling places.

It worked! Donn M. Roberts was sworn in as mayor of Terre Haute in January 1914. After that, though, things did not quite go as he had planned.

Less than two weeks after Roberts raised his hand to take the oath, a piece of paper was shoved into it. It informed Roberts that he was being indicted for election fraud. It seemed all of Terre Haute was talking, debating and taking sides over the trial. The trial began on March 28, 1914. The evidence against Roberts piled up. The smart money boys downtown and many others whispered that Roberts was in deep trouble. Soon, the word was that Donn was sure to be convicted. It was a foregone conclusion.

Then, a miracle. In May, the jury deliberated for only thirty minutes before announcing the shocking verdict of not guilty. Dark rumors spoke of rigging the jury, the way the election had been rigged. It did not matter. Donn Roberts soon announced that he would run for governor.

Trying to counter complaints that he was allowing the West End to run completely out of control, Roberts decided to take the Board of Public Safety members on a tour of the district in August 1914. He would show them it was not as bad as many said. He would show them that the stories of saloons flouting liquor laws and blasting music into the street and scantily clad women traipsing through the district were blown out of proportion. He chose a Sunday, thinking it would be the quietest day of the week. The group loaded into city cars and set out on the short trip into the bastion of sin. Things did not go as planned.

The first stop was at a "colored resort" at First and Eagle. The group drew quite a crowd. They were soon surrounded by Black prostitutes who had no idea who these White men visiting them were. The girls invited them into the house for a little Sunday fun. One tried to bum a cigarette from the mayor. Roberts was not amused. He threatened to "throw a bunch of black forms" in jail. They moved on.

The next stop was at Lockhart's Red Onion saloon. Again they drew a crowd of women offering various services to the boys. Although Lockhart had political pull, Roberts began arguing with him about women around the saloon. Lockhart roared back that he was just doing what others were allowed to do. He stunned Roberts by shouting back, "You can all go to hell. You're not going to make a goat out me."

Next stop was Tom Brady's saloon at Third and Cherry. Three barely dressed women lounged on a bench on the saloon's porch. There was another argument with an owner who spoke rudely to the mayor. The mayor then abruptly ended the tour.

If Roberts thought that things could not get much worse than on that sour Sunday, he was wrong.

Roberts enjoyed preening about as the mayor. He always felt he deserved his office because of his talents. He forgot that he also had a knack for making enemies. He did not suspect that two of them, one woman and one man, one newly made and another an old adversary, were making plans of their own.

Before the election, Roberts went to a legislative session in Indianapolis to gather support. He asked to meet Stella Stimson, a Terre Haute power in various reform-minded women's clubs in the state. He told her that he would be Terre Haute's next mayor and wanted the support of women. Stimson considered Roberts a "political tool." She told him that women wanted "good schools, good courts, streets safe from gamblers, wicked women and drunken men." Roberts disagreed.

Roberts replied that the "vote does not show that" and "the majority of Terre Haute citizens" don't want enforcement of vice laws. They wanted "all night and Sunday saloons, the segregated district and gambling." Stimson, fully aware of the West End precinct's reputation for fraud and Election Day violence, told him women would not support that. They better, was Roberts's reply. He would teach the women the rules. Stimson then organized 450 women to monitor the registration process for the election. It was this evidence that eventually led to Roberts's first indictment and acquittal.

An even more dangerous enemy was Joe Roach. Roberts and Roach hated each other. Joe Roach was an example of a man who completely turned his life around. Roach was known as a wild young man who was a "clever card shark and capable gunman." While serving time for murder, his remorse so impressed Indiana governor Thomas Marshall (later Woodrow Wilson's vice president) that Marshall pardoned him because of his "genuine desire to reform." Roach became a respected lawyer who served as both a defense attorney and a special prosecutor.

Stimson and Roach combined to get the federal government involved. Soon, a U.S. marshal was leading Roberts away to Indianapolis. This time, the trial was in federal court before a federal judge. Roberts was not alone. This time, 125 of his cronies, included Nugent, Hines and Clark, were also on trial. Among the other defendants were 26 city employees, 14 saloonkeepers, 21 bartenders and 2 boxers. In 1915, a total of 26 West Enders were charged. Most of the small fries received fines or minimal sentences. Roberts and 25 of his biggest henchmen, including Sheriff Dennis Shea and Judge Eli Redman, hit the big time—up to six years in Leavenworth. Of course, Roberts was impeached as mayor. Roach later moved to Indianapolis and then Chicago, where, among others, he represented members of the Al Capone gang.

They left behind the "problem" of the West End. Both the state and federal authorities told Terre Haute to clean up its act. Roberts was replaced as mayor by one-time crony James Gossom. Many were unsure why Gossom had managed to avoid indictment along with the others. Gossom didn't exactly jump into the situation. The first order to enforce the laws in the West End were issued while Gossom was away on a fishing vacation. While he was away, Charles Mancourt, the city controller, was acting mayor. He sent the police into the West End.

Under pressure, Gossom clamped down on saloons and gambling. He was in favor of relocating the red-light district. He was so successful in enforcing saloon laws that he upset Crawford Fairbanks, and soon there was a vote to impeach Gossom, but he survived. Although Gossom's crackdown hindered illegal liquor sales and gambling, he appears to have left the brothels pretty much as before.

THE SOCIAL HYGIENE MAN

The West End always had its share of homegrown con men, but it was a "tramp lawyer" who had already been run out of Gary and Indianapolis who stirred up the district in 1915.

Henry Price appeared in Terre Haute in late 1914. He carried with him a letter that said he was employed by the American Social Hygiene Association of Boston. His mission: clean up Terre Haute. He set himself up in the swanky Deming Hotel and said he was open for business. He even tried teaching "Sunday School" classes at the Temple Israel, an interesting concept.

He immediately tried to push his way into local politics. He particularly wanted to ingratiate himself with the Roberts regime, going so far as to represent some of Roberts's cronies on trial for corruption. But with Roberts and his crew boarding trains to Leavenworth, Price was left out in the cold.

Soon, rumors that Price was not what he appeared to be scurried through the city. It appeared that he had "gone into the reform business for other than purely uplift motives." He began approaching madams, seeking protection. (He must have figured that if Terre Haute officials could do it, why not him?) The madams decided to fight back. In a series of affidavits, they laid out Price's tactics.

Jessie Sheldon, who ran a brothel on North Third Street, said that the "alleged lawyer" first approached her after she made an appearance in police court. He then visited one of her girls in the brothel and pulled the madam aside. He said he could "insure her against molestation" by authorities. He also bragged that he was paid $1,000 by the hygiene group to clean up Terre Haute. Plus, he told her he got $25 a day plus a fee for each house he closed. Price summoned her to his office over a shoe store to make his pitch a few days later. If she did not want him to shut her down, she had to pay $25 a month, the first month in advance. Flustered, Sheldon said she did not have the money but would try to get it.

Margaret Clark and Daisy Kennedy, also from North Third, said Price represented them after meeting in the police station. He then began making almost nightly visits to their brothel. Price then wanted them to move to a house on Eagle that he would rent and furnish for them. He would become "a Number One" and loaf around the Deming Hotel and other places and send them clients. He later called Daisy and asked her to meet him without Margaret's knowledge. He told her he was soon going to be named the city court judge and have her brought before him. He would then send her to

Indianapolis to keep her away from other men because "he never saw a girl he thought of as much as he did" her.

Like all crafty con men, Price worked all the angles.

Myrtle Berry was the next madam to step forward. While Berry was shopping downtown with one of her girls, Price started flirting with the girl and arranged to meet her back at the house. While there, he posed as Donn Roberts's "personal friend" and said he had great influence downtown with the city administration. Taking her cue, Berry said she had a girl the police refused to register (perhaps because she was underage). Could Price help her? He could, he promised, for a fee. He went to the police and told them the girl was a friend of his from Gary, but they still refused to register her.

Following his pattern, the shady lawyer went to "visit" the girl at Berry's brothel. He did not have cash on him, so he borrowed money from Webb to pay her. He had the chutzpah to borrow money from a madam to pay the prostitute! He told Berry he would mail her the money.

There was a fourth affidavit, which the paper refused to publish because the details were "too unsavory."

When questioned, Price fell back on the "I'm being framed" argument and that he had received death threats. People were trying to run him out of town. He would show them he was on the up and up, but unfortunately he had yet to receive his official commission letter from the American Social Hygiene Association. The mail must be slow.

A letter soon arrived from the association, but not one Price was expecting. It said the association had never heard of Price and that he was not working for them. The jig was, indeed, up for him. He was disbarred and run out of town.

You would think those he bamboozled would have thought back eight years to another con man who fleeced the righteous flock. A man name Keen posing as a minister sent from Baptist Mission Church of London flounced into town announcing he was going to clean up sinful Terre Haute. After making his rounds and holding rallies for the faithful, he skipped town with their donations.

There were those genuinely committed to improving conditions in the district. Like Jane Addams, there were progressive women who tried to help those wishing it. One in particular was the Social Settlement house on North First. It offered the usual programs, like teaching women and girls about hygiene, cooking and cleaning, and offered education classes. It also worked among prostitutes, trying to help them escape the life or prevent them from entering it.

In 1915, a concerned policeman brought a young girl to the Settlement House. She had come to him to register as a prostitute "but was under age and he thought might be kept from this life." She was an innocent-looking young thing, pretty and "wearing a Juliet cap, long coat and eyeglasses." When questioned, she admitted that the cap and glasses had been loaned to her by a girl at a house on Second Street to make her look older. The youngster hoped to be registered and go to work in that house.

The girl was taken upstairs and locked in a bedroom with another underage girl who had also tried to go on the line. One of the social workers wished she could have overheard the conversation between two girls who both wanted to become prostitutes. Perhaps she then could come to a greater understanding of why it happened. Typically in such situations, the young girls were accompanied back to their homes. Often, they were met by teary-eyed parents relieved to have their daughters back. Other times, the social worker was castigated for returning her. In those cases, the parents had sent her to the West End to support the family.

Terre Haute also had a Florence Crittenton Home. Founded by a wealthy drug manufacturer and philanthropist and named in honor of his daughter, the homes were meant to reform "fallen women" and provide shelter for pregnant girls and their babies.

OUT OF BOUNDS

Prostitution was never wholly confined to the West End. There were always smaller brothels hidden away in the nooks and crannies of Terre Haute. They felt that, with attention focused on the district, their more low-key location would allow them to be left alone. Many of these were Black brothels in the more segregated neighborhoods, especially in the north and northeastern parts of town, like those on Grand Avenue and Spruce Street.

Just a few blocks east of the West End, another style of prostitution seems to have existed downtown. It appears to have been less brothel- and madam-oriented and geared more toward the pimp/streetwalker culture.

In 1912, one area downtown was known as the "Bull Pen" district. It was a series of buildings on the east side of Seventh Street between Wabash Avenue and Ohio Street. It featured furnished rooms rented by "men about town for the purpose of taking girls to them"—sort of a place for the upright men of the city to become horizontal with a special friend. They were "mixed use" buildings. The landlords would rent the two bottom floors to businesses.

The harder-to-rent spaces, such as the back, basement and third floor, were for the "Bull Pen Boys."

Just across Ohio Street (later the site of the Indiana Theater) was the Roberts Hotel. Once respectable when it was owned by his father, Donn Roberts turned it into a mini–West End. The hotel was part assignation house, part brothel and part bachelor quarters. A "negro clerk" was on duty twenty-four hours a day to check in guests to the assignation rooms. Guests were required to sign the register, no doubt using fictitious names. Bachelors were free to bring in their dates at any time.

The brothel normally had five girls in residence. Each had personal calling cards printed with their room numbers. The cards were passed out only to "gentlemen," so the girls were assured of a finer clientele. However, on slow nights, the girls sometimes took it to the streets. Roberts, of course, got his cut from the assignation rooms and rents. Naturally, the police looked the other way

Houses were not confined to downtown. Girls living on Fifth and Oak used their apartments to ply their trade. A well-known madam set up shop at Third and Farrington, across from a school. She defied any attempts by police to shut her down, a result of her political influence. She threatened to burn down the house of any neighbor who complained.

THE QUEEN II

Through all the turmoil, one person seemingly stood serenely above it and prospered.

In 1917, Edith Brown moved to what would become the palace among Terre Haute brothels. The two-story, sixteen-room building at 205 North Second was previously owned by Buster Clark. Buster, caught up in the election fraud cases, needed cash, so she got the place for a good price. Unusual for the period, it had three full baths. A new (or possibly old) swain was to help her furnish it in ostentatious style. A prominent, married Terre Haute furniture owner was smitten with Edith, and he made sure she had luxurious surroundings. People marveled at the house with its Oriental rugs, the best china and silver and ornate furniture.

Downstairs, there was madam Brown's private sitting room, a music room with a grand piano, a living room, a dining room and a spectacular bar. The bar itself was from the Prairie House, once Terre Haute's finest hotel. A mirror dominated the back wall of the barroom. It was eight feet tall, twelve

Canopy that once hung over the entrance to Edith Brown's house. *Vigo County Historical Society.*

feet long and had a gold-leaf frame. It was touted as the world's largest one-piece mirror, the claim not having been verified. It was said that it was made in France and had originally been part of the great 1893 Columbian Exposition in Chicago.

Visitors entering through the wrought-iron gate and walked through a door adorned with a Tiffany canopy. They might also note the formal garden. It was an elegant house that often catered to an elegant, wealthy clientele.

Though her house was classically furnished, Brown was also very modern. She drove one of the first electric cars in Terre Haute, and the brothel was thought to be the first place in the city to have a newfangled invention: a radio. She had a swimming pool installed in the fenced backyard, thought to be the first private pool in the city.

It was not just prostitution that filled the coffers of brothels. Selling alcohol was a major income source in many houses, sometimes bringing a higher profit margin than did the girls. They would sell beer for between fifty cents and one dollar a bottle, more than five times the price in saloons. The harder stuff was dearer still. Again, it was location, location, location. Brothels were one-stop convenience centers for vice. Gambling was on offer in some houses; eventually, drugs were added to the products on offer. A man could indulge several of his vices in one location. Go to the brothel, maybe gamble and drink a bit and then head upstairs with a girl. What more could a man want?

Despite the occasional, short-lived crackdowns, the West End carried on as before. It would take a world war to really shake up the red-light district.

Edith Brown girls. *Vigo County Historical Society*.

THE BIG CLEANSING

In August 1917, young Hilda Hants was working nights as a "Hello Girl" at the telephone company center on Wabash Avenue in Terre Haute. It was a time when all calls were operator-assisted. She worked in front of a huge switchboard, plugging in wires to connect calls.

One night, the switchboard literally lit up and buzzed constantly. The fevered calls were from prostitutes and madams to their local "customers." Hants and a friend listened in giddily as they connected the local soiled doves to some of the most prominent and upright men in the city. The prostitutes and madams informed the men that they needed money fast to finance their journeys to places like Chicago and Evansville until the heat was off the West End. Sometimes, their cajolery turned into threats of exposure if the local swains hesitated to come forward with the cash.

As they listened, Hants and her girlfriend conceived of the idea of going to the train station when their shift ended. This they did, likely flushed with the guilty pleasure of it all. Union Station was bustling. Black porters toted bags or loaded trunks onto carts headed for the baggage cars. Couples skulked behind pillars or gathered in dark corners. The girls watched nervous men surreptitiously slipping envelops into the lacquered fingers of fashionably dressed, painted-faced women. Hilda's friend pointed out two ministers she knew, as well as a couple of local politicians. For the girls who did not have sugar daddies to tap, West End king Buster Clark handed out money for train fares. That Buster was a gent.

The reason for the panic was a world war.

When the United States entered World War I in April 1917, the nation's army was vastly undermanned. That meant millions of men had to be trained as quickly as possible. Training camps blossomed across the country to meet this need. There was great competition among cities and towns to host the camps, which would greatly boost local economies. Terre Haute wanted one badly. Additionally, Indiana State would later form a Student Army Training Corps, a program in which officer candidates could combine military training with a college education.

With the thought of hundreds or thousands of healthy young men gathered together in one place, there were concerns about their off-duty pursuits. This led to a government push to shut down red-light districts over concerns of the spread of venereal diseases and clamp down on gambling and saloons. Government officials issued rules that forbade the location of any camp within five miles of places selling alcohol and within ten miles of prostitution and gambling. Terre Haute, of course, was well known for all three. The city had no chance of getting a camp unless something was done.

That is why there was such a panic in August 1917. The more experienced and stable madams, like Edith Brown, who had been through crackdowns tried to remain calm and figure out a way to ride out this latest storm. The madams of the low-level brothels and those without much political capital tried to think of a place elsewhere to set up business. Many girls immediately started packing their bags with their negligees, silk stockings and lacy underwear. They were mainly the ones who clogged the phone lines and the train station. An estimated three hundred girls left town within the first two weeks.

The West End was as empty as it had been in decades. But that did not mean prostitution had been erased from Terre Haute. Far from it. Edith Brown and perhaps seven or eight other madams kept their houses open, though in a much more low-key West End. The girls who stayed in town fanned out through the city. Some worked in under-the-radar houses, but most hit the streets. There were ongoing reports about the "small army" of streetwalkers and bar girls. Cheap hotels and rooms of assignation suddenly became very busy places. Gamblers, too, spread out through town. There were complaints that downtown Terre Haute had become one big gambling den.

Not all downtown merchants were happy with the shutdown. They saw their sales drop quite a bit. Buster Clark, a man who should know, said the West End added over $75,000 a month to the Terre Haute economy. In modern terms, that is equal to just over $1 million a month.

So, as Terre Haute ended 1917, it reverted in many ways to the chaos of 1906. The spread of vice throughout the city was just what the West End was supposed to prevent.

But the first golden age of the West End was over.

2

THE YO-YO YEARS

1918–23

It all depends on the people of Terre Haute how long it stays gone.
—*Terre Haute Citizen*

The era after World War I was one of seemingly constant ebb and flow in the West End.

Despite some officials crowing about closing it, the West End was beginning to thrive again by May 1918. The president of the Terre Haute Board of Safety lamented the fact. "I don't know what we are going to do with the old district. It is almost filled up again with women. They have been coming back for a while." He noted that at least eighty-one new prostitutes had made their way into the district. They claimed to be married to the men in the house or posed as cooks or maids. The most obvious of them served as barmaids in "soft drink parlors."

Indiana started Prohibition nearly two years before the rest of the nation. The legislature voted the state "dry" effective April 2, 1918. Saloons, bars and taverns were officially closed immediately. But they could reopen as soft drink parlors after obtaining a license to do so. The license fee helped make up some of the lost revenue from liquor license revenue.

Operated by many of the old saloonkeepers, the establishments carried on much as before. Whereas before they were selling alcohol during illegal hours, they were now selling illegal bootleg booze. Many still had ongoing gambling dens. With the closing of so many brothels, they became centers

'Es a Stubborn Lil' Feller

Cartoon lampooning Mayor Hunter's clean-up efforts. *Author collection.*

of prostitution. Girls hung around the soda parlors, working as barmaids or waitresses. Like the streetwalkers, these girls were often run by pimps. Still, many believed the parlors were one of the main reasons the brothels started to reopen.

Many blamed the resurgence on the new mayor, Charles Hunter, a Republican. It was not that he was thought to be corrupt, just ineffective and maybe a bit inept. Two years into his term, the *Saturday Spectator* stated that the mayor and his police force "stand convicted of incompetence." The article presented a list of their shortcomings. It blamed his administration for "official blindness" to illegal liquor sales, gambling, tawdry roadhouses and prostitution.

But Hunter did order a major vice raid in June 1918, and it was likely politically motivated. City Councilman Everett Raider had been trying to broker a deal with city officials that would allow the West End to reopen on a more limited scale. Raider seems to have had a very personal reason for this. One of the new girls in the district was from Indianapolis and called herself Edith Smith. She must have been an immediate hit, at least with the councilman.

It was well known that Raider was a regular visitor to the West End. So open were his trysts there that his wife went to Mayor Hunter to beg him to stop her husband from ruining his life. Hunter said he "talked to him with tears in my eyes but apparently to no avail." So, on a quiet Tuesday night, the raid was on.

Edith Smith's house on North Second was the first house on the list. Everett Raider was found enjoying Smith's companionship. He escaped out the back door but was caught next door in Brown's backyard. Raider took a seat in one of the paddy wagons, along with thirty other madams, girls and customers.

When asked directly if the raid was undertaken just to catch Raider, Hunter hesitated before saying, "No, not just that." The hesitation said it all. He then demanded that Raider resign or face impeachment.

Raider withstood the pressure for two months but finally resigned. He left Terre Haute for Indianapolis with Smith.

During Hunter's tenure, there would be token raids to assure the good citizens that something was being done about the district. But the raids were usually shrugged off after small fines were paid. Then it was back to business.

There were attempts at curbing some of the excesses of bawdy houses. Some of the girls at the lower-class houses were prone to stealing from their clients. While the man was distracted, a girl would grab what she could from his wallet, or another prostitute would slip into the room and make off with his cash. If the girls did not help themselves, there were plenty of men lurking in the streets who would. A man from the tiny village around Saint Mary-of-the-Woods College reported that he had been robbed of $120 in the West End. Why a man would saunter around the West End with the modern equivalent of over $1,500 in his pocket and expect to escape with most of his wad intact is unknown.

One commodity that grew more important in the West End during the period was drugs. Dealing narcotics became another profitable sideline for some West Enders. Federal agents began investigating a Terre Haute dope ring during World War I. As the investigation grew, as many as six different teams of agents worked on the case. It was a classic case of easily finding the small fries, the users and minor dealers. But officials were looking for the kingpin who controlled it all. They slowly began to suspect that the leader of the ring was the most powerful man in the West End and one of the most influential men in the city, Buster Clark. Buster "made or unmade more than one police official" and was vital to many political figures. Because of that, he had "practical immunity" from real prosecutions. Oh, he was arrested from time to time but had gone free due to lack of evidence or after paying minor fines. His only real jail time was as a teenager, when he was sent to the Indiana Boys School.

Buster was always willing to expand his business opportunities. And he needed some money in 1918. He was caught leading a silly scheme to steal car tires and resell them. It seemed a bit below Buster's skills, but he made the plunge and was caught. He had to pay a lot of money to lawyers and others to keep himself out of jail. He told cronies that it cost him $15,000 for fees and bribes. "I'm flat broke; worse than broke but it will not be long before I'm walking on velvet carpets again." Buster had made a lot of money but was an avid, though seldom lucky, gambler.

Looking around, he saw big profits in trafficking cocaine and narcotics. Now he had to find a supplier. Buster was highly trusted throughout the underworld. His word in business, it was said, was as "good as a banknote." He found his source in St. Louis. This early connection may be the reason the big city in Missouri was to play such a huge role in the future of the West End and Terre Haute.

Buster's brother-in-law Frank "Mickey" Meharry became a key part of the dope ring. He helped set up and run the pipeline. As a railroad employee, he got free travel passes on the railroads. He would sell or give the passes to a "snowbird" (slang for an addict) named Maurice "Cotton" Chase. Cotton would pick up the drugs in St. Louis and, acting as the "mule," carry the drugs to Terre Haute. Buster didn't even have to pay for the ticket that brought him riches.

The feds brought in their best investigator, Guy Broughton, to supervise the case. They kept moving up the hierarchy until they found the guy who would turn informant and bring them the head of Buster Clark. On Monday, April 12, 1920, they arrested not only Buster but also his wife, Lottie, at their "notorious" saloon and resort. Arrests of Mickey Meharry and others in the ring followed. The feds thought they had Clark two years earlier when they raided his saloon, but they came up empty, likely because Buster had been tipped off by someone in the Terre Haute police department.

The trial took place in Indianapolis in June. All the defendants pled guilty. Still, Buster was in good spirits, telling people he thought he might get six months in county jail. He could do that easy. He was shocked when the judge told him he would instead go to federal prison in Atlanta for between two and four years. To his credit, Buster begged the judge to give him the full four years in exchange for letting his wife go. It did no good. Lottie was sentenced to two years at the Indiana Women's Prison. Buster was also fined $5,000; Lottie was fined $2,500.

Mickey Meharry got one year and one day in Atlanta. The feds had an ace in the hole to pull against Mickey in case he was not convicted. They were going to charge him with defrauding the government. The government took over the railroads during the war; by selling or giving away railroad passes, he had broken federal law. The others received terms in county jails.

Buster and Mickey joined Terre Haute's most famous citizen in Atlanta. Socialist Eugene V. Debs had been there for years, unjustly prosecuted for opposing World War I.

It was a major victory for prosecutors. The case not only stopped the ring in Terre Haute, but the gang had also been thought to be distributing drugs throughout the Midwest. As Terre Haute was a major railway center serviced by railroads across the country, it was likely true. How many of the trips were free due to Meharry's connection is unknown.

The following year, a new mayor was elected. Republican Ora Davis was likely Terre Haute's most progressive and able mayor. He concentrated on attracting new businesses, making much-needed infrastructure improvements and adding amenities like Deming Park for the enjoyment of citizens. He was no supporter of the West End. Policing it became steadier, but for the most part he had more important things to do for the city. As long as things remained under control and no overt problems arose from the district, he tended to other things.

Davis was so highly regarded that he was touted as the next governor. Unfortunately, he ran afoul of the all-powerful Ku Klux Klan in the state. His open anti-Klan stance basically doomed his candidacy. And though the Klan touted its all-American, Protestant, clean-living tenets, it does not seem to have made any major practical steps to close the West End down. In fact, business in the West End seemed to boom when the Klan held its massive rallies in Terre Haute.

PIMPS

William Bunkley was a tired man when he headed to bed at his West End house on November 9, 1920. Whatever he had done that day, it was probably not entirely legal. As they say, he and his brothers were "well known to the police." We don't know if he stirred when his wife, Mildred, crept into their bedroom. Probably not, as he was known to like a drink or two. We also don't know if his sleeping companion, a woman name Pattie Finnegan, was restless enough to be aware of the other woman in the bedroom. But, if not, she was aware of it a second later, when Mildred put a revolver to her husband's head and pulled the trigger. We don't know if the frightened Finnegan jumped up to try to run away or raised her hand in self-protection. We do know that Mildred Bunkley shot Pattie in the hand.

Mildred told police her husband forced her into prostitution and into robbing her clients. He was her pimp. She could not take it anymore. She believed he was also Finnegan's pimp. The story caused a stir, particularly because Bunkley was Black and Mildred and Pattie were White. Even then, there was a prevailing belief that Black men sought out White women with the intent of forcing them into prostitution. The jury (unusual for the era, it included two women) must have been sympathetic. Instead of the first-degree murder she was charged with, it convicted Mildred only of manslaughter.

She served slightly more than the two-year minimum sentence. The general feeling was that she had done the city a favor.

William Bunkley was called "a man of the lowest type, but he lived a life of ease off from the earnings and stealings of women." It is hard to gauge the extent of pimp culture in the West End. One report claimed there were over two hundred men in the district living "off the immoral earnings" of women. That seems exaggerated, but no doubt there was a very large number of pimps in the West End. Most often "their girls" walked the street or congregated in saloons or dance halls. However, there were also a lot of pimps who "sold" the girls to brothels and took their earnings. Twenty years later, a madam told of some girls who worked for pimps on their days off.

New Neighbors

There was a positive change in the West End during these years.

There were always "ordinary" people living within the West End's boundaries. They were mostly dirt poor and clustered in the northern and eastern parts of the district. The 1900 census showed they had jobs like chicken pluckers, overalls folders and shirt packers. There was even a clairvoyant.

Even more families moved in during the uncertain times. Property owners, fearing that the days of high rents paid by madams and others during the good times were over, began lowering rents The idea of renting good houses at reasonable rates drew in more working-class families. Children played in the streets where muggers once skulked. This group of newcomers would help form the core of the West End community of the future.

3

SETTLING IN

The Second Golden Age and Beyond

The second golden age began in the middle of the Jazz Age. It was the era of flappers, racoon coats and the Charleston. The whole country seemed to be seeking a release from everyday life and the aftermath of a world war and a devastating epidemic. It was a time to let go and enjoy life. And let go they did. The West End returned with a vengeance. A 1943 report estimated that there were one hundred brothels operating in 1928, the year before the stock market crash brought on the Great Depression. That is likely an exaggeration, unless the report was counting the bootleg saloon joints, dance halls and soda parlors that had girls on offer. Future mayor Lee Larrison visited the West End at least twice a week, delivering and selling cosmetics to the girls. His estimate of fifty to sixty houses during the 1930s is more reliable. Even so, it showed that the West End was back.

The second golden age was also during Prohibition, which was an idiotic attempt at social engineering that left permanent scars and perpetual problems in its wake. One madam recalled that Prohibition was a great time for the West End. Money came in hand over fist, both from illegal booze and the houses. Money was flowing, and good times roared through the district. It brought new people and new forces into Terre Haute and the West End, particularly from St. Louis and Chicago. Gangs battled over the Terre Haute turf. The St. Louis connection was the most felt in the West End.

One of the most important St. Louis imports was a young woman named Maryann Lewis. She would run West End brothels from 1925 until 1970, longer than any other madam. She wasn't there in the beginning, but she was at the end. Hers was one of the final three houses shut down when the red-light district was closed forever. She witnessed more of life in that corner of sin city than just about anyone.

Lewis was born in St. Louis in 1902. After being sexually harassed by most of the bosses she worked for and hating her job in a shoe factory, she decided there was more to life than that. She wanted to be her own boss and was an admitted "thrill seeker." She got her start in the business in 1922 in St. Louis by turning her house into a house of assignation, renting out rooms to streetwalkers so they had a place to bring their johns. It was "pretty fast money" to rent out the room for fifteen minutes. It was a business plan that taught her well about men and money.

She passed through Terre Haute while traveling to Detroit with a girlfriend. She was taken by the beauty of the scenery, and when they passed through the West End, she was thrilled by the atmosphere of the place, the excitement and "music everywhere." Maryann loved music. She told her friend that this was a place she wanted to live. She moved to Terre Haute in 1925 and tried to set up business.

The place she wanted belonged to Jack Hines. It was a double house just down the block from Edith Brown. She was denied her attempts to rent it. The district was a bit "cliquey." It did not greet newcomers with open arms, but that did not stop Lewis. She was rebuffed by several people when she tried to rent the house to open her brothel. She was forced to rent a cottage outside of the West End to set up an assignation house. The snoopy landlord kept intruding, and she started to look in the West End again.

This time, she went directly to Jack Hines, telling him she really wanted to rent that house. When he asked why she hadn't rented it before, she told him that someone kept her from it. One of those against her was Dot Meharry, Buster Clark's sister. Hines rented it to her, and Maryann's long life as a West End Madam was underway. Within two years, she had married Mickey Meharry after his divorce from Dot. Mickey was a fascinating man, and he and Maryann would form quite a team. More on that side of the story later.

Maryann Meharry was a unique individual. She was very open-minded and down to earth. She was a very forthright person. She had a sharp mind for business and a questioning intellect. She loved books, and they were always a feature in her life. Both her home and her brothel reflected the feelings of Welsh writer Anthony Powell, who titled one of his novels *Books Do Furnish a Room*. Maryann would become the chronicler, the memory, of the West End. She and her stories embody the human side of the West End.

Maryann Meharry was not welcomed with open arms. Other madams were not thrilled with more competition. They tried to prevent her getting business and tried to keep the better-looking girls from moving to Meharry's house. Maryann felt it was also a personality conflict. They considered her "stuck up." Unlike other madams, she neither smoked nor drank, nor was she into carousing. The only thing she had in common with the others was the business. She preferred keeping to herself and reading. It took nearly ten years for her to become more or less accepted. Interestingly, her closest friend in the West End was another madam who kept to herself and above the fray, Edith Brown.

Meharry arrived during the revival of the West End. By the coming of World War II, it would once again contain around sixty houses and hundreds of girls. It would also change from primarily a vice district to a neighborhood. The names of certain madams would once again become well known throughout Terre Haute. People knew who Kate Adair, Nell Bandy and Joan Lee were.

Like other places, Terre Haute and Vigo County tried to ignore Prohibition. They were, after all, home to large breweries and distilleries. Their now-unemployed workers knew how to make booze of all kinds. Stills sprouted like untended weeds in the area. Even the most conservative estimates acknowledge that there were more than two hundred stills cooking in the county. The true figure over time is closer to one thousand.

Gangs in St. Louis and Chicago looked to Terre Haute for potential partners, customers and suppliers. It was not always an amicable encounter among them. Gang warfare did occasionally erupt in the streets of Terre Haute, and several murders took place between rival bootleggers. Very little of that chaos seemed to have seeped into the West End. It is almost as if it was regarded as a shared space. The gangs were more interested in selling their bootleg booze, setting up gambling dens and enjoying the pleasures of the district.

Prohibition brought another St. Louisan to prominence in Terre Haute. Joe Traum, along with brother Jake "Blackie" Traum, said they were part of the Egan (also Eagan) Rats gang from St. Louis. Whether there really was such a gang or the Traums gave themselves the moniker is unknown. Joe Traum later told Maryann Meharry that they had just made up the name to frighten people. Also in doubt was whether Traum was sent "officially" as an emissary of St. Louis gangs or came on his own. No matter the truth, the Traums and their Missouri brethren would considerably ratchet up the violence around Terre Haute during their reign, though it all seems to have taken place outside of the West End.

Another member of the St. Louis gang was an old classmate of Meharry's. Homer Wright was a tough man. Even the other gang members feared him, including Joe Traum. Meharry had a soft spot for him. They were lifelong friends. Whenever Wright came to Terre Haute to pick up a load of bootleg whiskey, he would park at Meharry's. Someone would pick up his car, load him up and return it to Meharry's. He would then head out.

After Wright was killed in a hijacking, the madam was sure she knew who murdered her old friend. Meharry had some visitors to the saloon and brothel. She was well acquainted with Traum and his gang. They often drank and gambled in her husband's saloon and visited her brothel in the district. After the murder, two of Traum's henchmen, Tom Fagan and "Crooked Neck" Crane, came into Mickey's saloon. They asked her if she had heard the bad news about Homer. They then asked if they could wash up. Maryann told them they could but that they had to surrender their guns, like always. They always had, but this time they refused to hand them over, possibly because Maryann could smell that they had been recently fired. Seeing the look in their eyes, she decided that maybe they could keep their guns this one time.

She went to her grave believing that Tommy and Crooked Neck murdered Homer Wright.

Prohibition brought a lot of noted visitors to the West End. The most famous were Al Capone and John Dillinger. Capone spent a lot of time in Terre Haute checking on his bootlegging and gambling interests. He would spend a night in the best brothels while his souped-up roadster was being tuned up by a wizard mechanic across the bridge in West Terre Haute. Dillinger visited the district but stayed elsewhere. His favored place to hole up was the second floor of a tavern owned by a friend on South First, about four miles from the West End. The nation's most famed bank robber actually owned a house on Fenwood Avenue on the east side of town. He had a Muncie, Indiana madam buy it for him under her name. It was used as a hideout for some of his gang.

More than a few famous entertainers wound their way into the West End. Terre Haute was part of two different vaudeville circuits and had several theaters that hosted traveling plays. In was not unusual for famous entertainers to surreptitiously sneak through the back doors of the finer brothels. John Kent Lamb, former executive vice-president of the Terre Haute Chamber of Commerce, said it best when he noted that the West End was the place men came "not to be seen in places like where they might be picked up" by police

But the majority of those visiting the West End were ordinary men. And 90 percent of them were from out of town. The West End was indeed a sex tourism destination, drawing men from across the country. They would make furtive trips to the exotic district. But there were locals who paid regular visits to "the line," as it was known. Truckers and railway men made it part of their trips through town. Local factory workers were among the most regular clients. On Fridays and Saturdays after payday, they would go as a group, mainly to the middle or cheap houses, though sometimes they splurged at Meharry's, Kate Adair's and Rose Moon's houses.

Kate Adair was another St. Louis woman who became a force. Born Kate Hartman in 1883, she led an interesting life before coming to Terre Haute. She married a man named Joe Gersbacher at age sixteen. Within a year, she was the mother to a young son, also named Joe. The marriage dissolved quickly after that. When and why she came to Terre Haute is a mystery. By 1917, she was running an illegal resort in the West End. She also found time to marry a man named Jesse Filkins in Brazil, Indiana, in 1917. Evidently, that marriage was shorter than her first one. Jesse appears to have disappeared from her life within a year or two. She was arrested in January 1918 at her resort and listed as Kate Filkins (aka Kate Hartman). There is no mention of her son being with her. He may have stayed behind with his father, who had remarried, or lived with family.

After her arrest, she left town and returned to St. Louis for a short period. In September, she was listed as Kate Filkins and living with her son, Joe, when he registered for the World War I draft. (He would again list her, as Kate Adair, as the person to contact on his World War II draft registration form.) By 1920, she owned a "restaurant" on Eagle Street. Living with her was a twenty-three-year-old girl listed as a "roomer." Though Kate described herself as married, there was no sign of Jesse Filkins. Two years later, she was married to James Adair, who was operating a soft drink parlor. They became another husband-wife team in the West End.

As Maryann Meharry's efforts show, location was a very important factor in the West End. Corner lots were the prime locations. They commanded attention for those entering the district. The lower-class houses tended to be in the middle of blocks. The worst brothels were situated in alleys or in the darker sections of the district.

Like the rest of American society, there were definite class divisions,

Edith Brown's elegant brothel was an example of a "parlor house." These were houses that sought to offer an experience, not just a bedroom to conduct the business of pleasure. They featured elegant foyers and tastefully furnished parlors with Oriental carpets, overstuffed chairs and lounges. It was all meant to give the house an air of refined respectability. The ambience madams wanted was similar that of a gentleman's club.

Here men could gather, have a drink, smoke a good cigar and converse on matters of the day if they wished. Some houses offered live music or at least a Victrola. It was a relaxed, convivial atmosphere that slowly gave rise to a feeling of sexual tension. Then, when the madam sensed the time was right, the girls would be brought in. They were elegantly dressed, not cavorting in lingerie. They were attractive; only the young, prettiest girls would do in such a house. They often spoke with the men, perhaps joined them for a drink. After that, the decisions were made, pairs joined up to go upstairs to nicely furnished bedrooms with real beds, not creaking single beds or tawdry cots. It was class all the way.

Meharry's house could also be called a parlor house. Her brick house at 214 Cherry was special to her. The oval-shaped front door was surrounded by lead-glass panels. The oak storm doors were covered by wrought-ironwork. They had been rescued from the mansion of a very prominent Terre Haute family, the Minshalls. The "M" monogram on the door was the added touch.

Guests entered to find a staircase on the left and two rooms on the right. The first was a parlor, the second was the music room. Down the hall was the "common room," a large space with a polished hardwood floor. A previous madam used it as a dance hall. To the left was a kitchen, dining room and small parlor, and another parlor was near the staircase. The parlors offered privacy to prominent Terre Hauteans and other noted visitors who wanted privacy during their visits.

The second floor was the "business floor." It contained five nicely furnished bedrooms and a bathroom. Meharry's house was probably second only to Edith Brown's. There were plenty more below in the pecking order. The deciding factors in the caste system were price, quality of girls and amenities.

The lowest of the low were called "cribs." These were buildings that contained a series of very small rooms, usually with a door that opened onto the street. They had a "small bed and a table with a wash basin." They were for pure functionality, not show. Very little money was exchanged, and the girl and client quickly went about their business. It was literally "slam bam, thank you ma'am." It was vice built on quantity. The only way these girls, often called "dollar girls," could make any money was by volume. And they could not be picky about the men who wanted to buy them for fifteen minutes. Most often, the houses were operated by men (pimps) who provided little or no protection for the girls. No evidence suggests the cribs were present in the West End unless it was during the Jockey Alley days.

In general, cribs and dives were run by men. They could be saloonkeepers who allowed girls to use their back rooms or head upstairs to spartan rooms. They also had what were called wine rooms or women's rooms, which allowed prostitutes a place to serve as "hostesses." Even if these girls did not manage to entice a client upstairs, they were given a cut on the profits of the liquor they sold.

Meharry thought the elements that helped determine the status were "furnishings, housekeeping, intelligence of the girls, their wardrobe and their speaking ability." She thought the best houses in the district were hers, Edith Brown's and those run by Kate Adair, Jesse Hartman and Joan Lee. The higher standard of all those determined the prices charged, and costs were the ultimate factor in the status of the house. This made them initially five-dollar to ten-dollar houses and twenty-plus-dollar houses in later years.

Below that were the brothels that ranged from four-dollar places down to the lowest dives, where the charge might only be fifty cents. Meharry might have added hygiene to her list. Girls at the best houses were required to bathe or shower between customers. At the "bowl and basin" houses, many of the girls literally took what were known as a "whore's bath," which meant washing only her genitals and under her arms.

There was another new addition to the West End in 1925 that was applauded by all. Terre Haute had been looking for a site for a boy's club for several years. The effort was spearheaded by Florence Gulick. After looking at many properties, the committee bought a house at 220 North Third for $6,000. The house belonged to a local grocer named Salem Nasser, who sold it at $500 below value because he supported the cause. It was not the location they really wanted, but the other properties considered were too expensive.

The house they most wanted was Edith Brown's brothel. Brown had said she was willing to sell, but her property was simply too expensive. There were two intriguing points about the Florence Gulick Boy's Club. First, it was located well within the boundaries of the West End. In fact, it was surrounded on all sides by brothels. If the district was as dangerous and evil as portrayed, why place a club for inquisitive and suggestible boys in the middle of temptation?

The second point was Edith Brown's willingness to sell her palace. Was she looking to get out of the business after twenty-five very successful years? Was it because she had an even more elaborate place in mind? Was it because she had married gambler, bootlegger and vice boss Eddie Gosnell the previous year and was contemplating a new life? That would be intriguing, except that she and her new husband never lived together. She spent Thursday nights at Eddie's club north of Terre Haute but returned home the next morning. As always, the enigmatic Edith Brown kept her thoughts deep within.

Brown continued to be a huge supporter of the club. She provided money each year for a Christmas dinner for the boys who attended the club. When they were trying to raise the funds to build a gymnasium, Brown arranged for each madam to donate $25 and each girl $1 to the cause. She left the club $5,000 in her will. As the club director said, "She was a nice lady."

Brown continued to operate the best little whorehouse in Terre Haute. Her moneyed guests would be entertained by live music and sipped the best liquor, even during Prohibition. She hosted elegant parties on many Sundays. The guests sometimes included the wives of prominent men. Everyone was required to wear formal dress. Not all the male visitors partook of all of the pleasures of the house. Many just stopped by for the elegant surroundings and interesting conversations. Among them was Terre Haute businessman and poet Max Erhmann of *Desiderata* fame.

It was a shame that a house of such beauty was the site of an ugly, atrocious event. Brown's sugar daddy remained very much a part of her life after she married Eddie Gosnell. Her special "friend" still squired her around to dinner and the theater and attended her soirees. He provided her with fancy cars. But he made the last mistake of his life while visiting the house in 1929. Probably under the influence of alcohol, he began a very public argument with Brown that ended with him slapping her face. Perhaps before he had time to realize what he had done, Eddie Gosnell rushed at him. Gosnell gave him a vicious, brutal beating. The man was rushed to the hospital, where he died a few days later. All that was left behind of the incident were rumors. Gosnell was not arrested, even though he had beaten a man to death. It was a matter of honor, some said; a crime of passion in defense of a fair lady. The French would understand such things.

The women the johns chose from were beautiful. Brown made sure they were elegantly dressed. They had to wear gowns. Even when they went out, they had to be nicely dressed. A man recalled them coming into his father's grocery store, and they were all sedately dressed. From their demeanor and clothing, one would have never guessed their profession. They were good customers who paid in cash. Since they were allowed to have pets, some of them had the butcher grind round steak for their dogs.

Madam Edith Brown's "palace." *Vigo County Historical Society.*

Madam Brown's girls were always safe. She made them register both their real names and "brothel" names with the health department and be given a clean bill of health before she hired them. All prostitutes were supposed to be checked at least monthly, but some of the sleazier brothels ignored this dictum. The prostitutes were a bit coddled in the good houses. They were expected to keep their own rooms, but maids were available. Brown's domestic staff included several maids, a cook and a gardener-handyman. For all this, the girls had to follow the rules, be polite and maintain a sense of decorum.

One of the oddest moments in the West End occurred in July 1935. A strike at a local plant, Columbian Enameling, had led to only the second general strike in the United States. The city was placed under martial law, and the National Guard was called in to quell possible violence. Strike supporters marched through Terre Haute streets trying close down all the businesses in town. Many complied.

One day, a group of strikers, baseball bats in hand, entered the West End shouting, "close up, close up." Meharry hurried to her porch and asked them what the hell was going on. "The union, the unions. Support the union." Meharry correctly informed them that "nobody belongs to the union here." "It doesn't matter, you gotta support the union." Discretion being the better part of valor, Meharry decided it best to close her door. She didn't want to see a Louisville Slugger smashing her leaded glass. Eventually, things calmed down, and the strikers decided that, as long as they were there, they might as well have some fun. Leaving the front doors of saloons and brothels alone, they headed for the back doors to taste the delights inside.

The Struggling Years

The end of Prohibition and the lingering effects of the Great Depression ended the second golden age. Like the rest of the country, the West End suffered the doldrums. Brothels were good barometers of the economy. Fewer men came to the house, or they came less frequently. They haggled about the prices for the first time, trying to get the madam or girls to give them a "discount." The bad times also brought about a big change in what the girls were willing to "do" for money.

When Maharry interviewed girls before the Depression, she would ask what they were willing to do for the money. If they said they would do things outside the norms of the time, she would not hire them. But with times so tight, she found the girls willing to go further than before. As she said, "You could go to bed natural or unnatural." Unnatural became more common. She didn't like it, but it was up to the girl, unless Meharry thought it was too far. This willingness to go beyond what the girls were comfortable with "broke out like measles" among the prostitutes. Suddenly, things previously thought taboo, like anal sex, bondage and S&M, became just another part of the routine. It took an added toll on many of the girls, but they did what they had to do to survive.

In the midst of the doldrums, the district had yet another mayor to deal with. Samuel Beecher Sr. took office in 1936. Each new mayor was something of a crapshoot for the West End. Each would pledge to do something about the vice district to get elected, but the voters never knew how much he would follow through on his campaign promises. It was always a test of the political pull of West End powers and the will of the mayor.

It did not take long for Beecher and the West End to clash. Let's call the issue "Window Shade-Gate." During the campaign, Beecher vowed to make the brothels keep their window shades down, to prevent girls from exhibiting themselves. He issued the order when he took office, and police were sent to make sure the shades were indeed down. This caused a group of West End bosses—called the "men making money without working guys" by a local paper—to storm into the office of the police chief to demand that shades be opened again. Soon, the word went out that the shades could stay up. This up-or-down tug-of war caused great irritation within the police force. It got so bad that officers were afraid to be seen talking together. A wag noted that the police were so frightened they "were afraid to open their mouths to wash their teeth." The shades mainly stayed up for people to gawk at the girls.

There was some doubt about whether Beecher would keep his pledges. It was made worse when the city offices had to move while a new city hall was being built. Interestingly, the old Hook School building was chosen. It bordered the northern edge of the West End. Critics began calling the West End "Beecherville," because the mayor's office was nearly surrounded by brothels, saloons and gambling dens.

Beecher was accused of merely making a show of enforcing the law, because he wanted to become the judge of the city court when his term was over. But he turned out to be made of sterner stuff than many Terre Haute mayors. He did not believe in a segregated area of vice, but he was stuck with it. He continued to crack down on the West End, but his main target was gambling, not prostitution. In 1937, he had gambling dens and saloons with slot machines raided. Attempts to close brothels were made, but as usual, the house crept back in later.

It was noted that the raids showed that many of the prostitutes arrested were from out of town. They came to Terre Haute to escape the heat in their old locales. Just as the West Enders escaped to other cities, Terre Haute became the destination for others looking for a soft landing spot to wait out enforcement in their areas.

Terre Haute had a new mayor in 1940. Republican Vern McMillan owned a sporting-goods store and thought himself an important figure in the city. Maryann Meharry had unpleasant dealings with McMillan and considered him the most hypocritical of all the mayors she dealt with. She recalled the times he was campaigning and would come to her place or Mickey's bar, sit on a stool and blather on about his virtues. And he was cheap, the type who would nurse a Budweiser and move on down the bar when it came his turn to buy a round for the others. She also hated how he always took credit for closing the West End during World War II. That honor belonged to the government.

The beginning of the war led to a brief boom in the West End. For a time, it was like the old days. Soldiers and travelers flooded Terre Haute. Meharry recalled groups of servicemen visiting her house. Perhaps only one of them would go upstairs with a girl. The others would sit in the parlor, drinking Coke, chatting with girls and listening to music. It was a sort of adult USO for the visiting military.

But it didn't last long. In April 1942, Maryann Meharry received a phone call from Milton Levinson, a prominent downtown businessman. He told her to come to his office that day, not the next. She hurried to meet him at his clothing store. He told her in confidence that a representative from the government had told a group of business owners that they were going to be closing the West End within days. Whatever income they got from the district was going to vanish. Levinson wanted her to help him get money the girls owed him before they were pushed out of town.

A bit shaken, she went back to the house and called in the girls to tell them to settle any debts they had right away. When the knock came on the door, they would be forced to leave. The knock came the next morning at the hands of police lieutenant William Searcy. Meharry was still in bed when her housekeeper told her the cops wanted to see her. They did not take "no" for an answer when the housekeeper told them her boss was not up yet. "Get her up," was their command.

They told her to close down immediately. She had twenty-four hours to shut her doors and evict the girls.

Once again, the reason was the military trainees attending special courses at Indiana State and Rose Polytechnic. Indiana State trained pilots and offered other programs for the U.S. Navy. Secret Service and other agency personnel came to Terre Haute to see that the orders to close down the West End were carried out. They observed over three hundred girls taking their belongings and leaving the district.

Did they all stay away for the duration? Not exactly.

By August 1942, many of the girls had "drifted back from the taverns and residential districts they had taken abode." The reoccupation took place quietly. Curtains were kept closed and eyes peeped out from doors to scrutinize visitors. It was not as full as the old West End, but it was going strong.

Since McMillan's police force was ignoring it, the state police raided the district on a Sunday. They ended up arresting twenty-six girls, five madams and George Gillette for operating houses of ill-fame. There were other houses operating, but they had been tipped off about the raid and went dark. Gillette had a crafty lawyer who got him off on the charge. One of the girls arrested at Gillette's antiques-filled, Oriental-carpeted house convinced the court that it was a "tourist home," not a brothel!

After that, that the West End was very quiet. Everybody was much more circumspect, except for Joan Lee and her girls, who continued to exhibit themselves in the windows. Only a few houses stuck it out. Maryann Meharry usually only kept one girl working and resorted to renting to male boarders. The district continued to help the war effort. It led many successful scrap drives.

4

PEOPLE OF THE WEST END

Being stranded ten days on the ice of western Greenland can affect a person for the rest of their life. Such, seemingly, was the case with Carl Bauman.

The slender young welder from Terre Haute was the flight engineer on a B-17 called *My Gal Sal* being sent to England in June 1942. The plane was named after the song written by Bauman's fellow Terre Hautean Paul Dresser. The plane was part of a thirteen-plane flight to ferry B-17s to England. The long flight required refueling stops in Goose Bay, Labrador, Greenland and Iceland. If all went well, they could be routine flights. But not for those who took off on June 26, 1942.

The flight ran into heavy cloud banks at they left Canada. Five pilots opted to return to Goose Bay. Five luckily managed to locate the airbases in Greenland. *My Gal Sal* was among the not-so-lucky three to be forced to ditch.

As the plane approached Greenland, one of the engines failed, likely because fuel was running out. Making things worse, just then, the navigation system failed as a snowstorm blinded them. The twenty-two-year-old pilot had no choice but to try a dangerous forced landing on the icecap. He made it.

Carl Bauman was one of the thirteen airmen to crawl out of the broken plane. Miraculously, all had survived. To celebrate, they all sang a rousing chorus of "My Gal Sal." But they found themselves on a seemingly endless expanse of ice with not a hint of another human anywhere in sight. Taking stock, they discovered the only food on the plane were a "dozen sandwiches and a box of Baby Ruths" candy bars. Their only chance of being discovered was to get their radio working and call for help. Ingeniously, the crew chopped off the propellers. Using what little fuel remained, they ran the engine to power the radio.

Luckily, their radio distress message was picked up the following day. Six search planes were tasked with finding the downed bomber. Food and supplies were air-dropped to the crew. One request the planes could not honor was to "drop us a couple of blonds." Deep, undulating crevasses and bad weather prevented rescuers from reaching the stranded airmen on foot or through the air. Bauman and his mates could only wait and hope.

On July 3, a float plane spotted a temporary lake that had formed on the icecap by melting snow. The plane landed to drop off a rescue party, which used life rafts to make it to the shore, and then took off again to drop more food and supplies to the *Sal*. The weather still prevented rescuers from reaching the plane. Finally, on July 5, the searchers made it to the crash site. Donning snowshoes, everyone made the thirteen-mile trek to the base camp through horrible weather. They finally arrived, exhausted, at 9:30 a.m. on July 6. Two flights carrying eight men each took them to the air base. The crew was given ten days' rest.

Yes, events like that can change a man.

Born in 1921, Carl Bauman enlisted in the army air corps on New Year's Eve 1941, twenty-four days after Pearl Harbor. He was eager to serve his country. Six months later, he found himself on a desolate Greenland ice field. After arriving in England, Carl sent his parents a package containing letters, photos and drawings. He told his mother to make sure she preserved the materials. In August, the *Terre Haute Star* published an article about Carl and his adventures. His mom kept that for him, too. Carl would want that when he came home.

Bauman returned to Terre Haute after being discharged in 1945. Within a few years, his first wife had divorced him and took their child with her. Maryann Meharry was Carl's friend. She blamed the war and the woman he married during World War II for his troubles. Both, she believed, "contributed to his downfall." Carl's ex-wife quickly married another man after the divorce and then left her new husband for the husband of one of her friends. Carl took it hard.

He later remarried. He went back to work as a laborer and welder—when he had a job, that is. Many years, he had no work. He lived in the West End and took day jobs or stints as a bartender. Sometimes, he swept up the saloons after the crowd had gone home.

Carl Bauman kept this article about the exploits on *My Gal Sal. Author collection.*

When *LIFE* magazine did a feature on the *My Gal Sal* and its survivors in 1965, it found Carl on a stool in a West End tavern, "out of a job and down on his luck." He did odd jobs around the tavern to pay for his drinks. Though only forty-four, he had the worn, haggard look of a man two decades older. A large cyst ballooned from the bridge of his nose. It bothered him, he said, but he was afraid to "go to the hospital." He asked about his comrades from *My Gal Sal*. One had died in the war, but the other eleven had made something of their lives. Bauman's face twisted into a small wry smile as he mulled unspoken thoughts. He did not have much to his name, but he always kept a "newspaper clipping about a long-ago arctic adventure" with him. The article featured a picture of the twenty-one-year-old airman, looking slim, youthful, athletic (he was an accomplished gymnast) and hopeful. It also had photos and a drawing Bauman had sent in a letter to his parents recounting his ordeal.

Less than a year after the *LIFE* article appeared, Bauman died of cirrhosis of the liver. The drink had finally killed him. Legal papers filed after his death stated that his estate was "of no value." Carl was soon forgotten by most. But Maryann Meharry remembered him. And many years later, so did accomplished singer-songwriter David Hanners in his song about Carl.

MY GAL SAL

My name is Carl Bauman, they just call me Junior
Served on the crew of the bomber My Gal Sal
Damn-near froze to death stranded in the Arctic
Buy me a drink and I'll tell you 'bout it now

Flying Fortress was a fine ship, Pride of Seattle
All of us itchin' to give Hitler what-for
Headed off to England to join the Mighty Eighth
We hit lousy weather just out of Labrador

Ralf Stinson was the pilot; he was a good man
But when nature's got your number ain't much you can do
He said, "Boys, we're goin' down, take your crash positions"
We ditched on Greenland ice and waited for rescue

I lived through that and made it through the war
Saw boys blown to atoms over Germany
Come home to Terre Haute, found myself a gal
Wasn't married long before she walked out on me

Some men adjusted fine, picked up where they left
Ralf became a doctor, I heard somebody say
Some of us were like that bomber in the clouds
Engines droning on 'though we had lost our way

Not every casualty of war is buried 'neath a white cross
In some graveyard on some foreign shore
Some of us came home, we'd just lost our bearings
Life stopped making sense 'bout 1944

So now I sweep this tavern, they pay me in wine
Fact is there ain't much that I can do
Now I'll take that shot and I'll also need a chaser
And I hate to drink alone so pour one for you

My name is Carl Bauman, they just call me Junior
I'll sleep it off, tomorrow is another day
I feel like My Gal Sal up there in the clouds
Engines droning on 'though she had lost her way

The One-Eyed Bartender

Everyone loved George Washington Harris. Known as Sody, he had the kind of personality that seemed to draw people to him. He had black hair and gray eyes that seemed to have a sly tinkle about them. But just as he drew people, drugs drew him. He was an addict and a dealer. He was twice arrested as part of a narcotics ring supplying Terre Haute with heroin, morphine and opium. He didn't start out that way.

Born in Effingham, Illinois, in 1879, he left home to fight in the Spanish-American War in 1898. He likely fought in Cuba, as he was discharged in Florida in 1900. His discharge papers described him as a fine soldier.

After the war, he settled in Springfield, Illinois, for a while. He tended bar and likely ran gambling games in the back room. It was there he began doing drugs. Supposedly, it started with smoking hop (marijuana) with showgirls who worked the burlesque houses in town. By 1910, he had drifted into the West End. He became something of a fixture there, easily mixing in with all sorts of people. A friend said he "had a personality that made everybody love him."

But Sody was an addict. His habit came to dominate his life.

Sody liked the way that drugs made him feel awfully good. It was easy enough to find drugs in Terre Haute in those days. During the early part of the century, the city was a center of opium production. Entrepreneurs even imported Chinese workers to brew up batches of the drug in a storefront on Wabash Avenue. Besides, drugs like morphine, heroin and cocaine were legal until 1913. You could go to the local drugstore to buy your fix or even order them from the Sears & Roebuck catalogue. No problem. Have them delivered right to your door.

The likeable Sody dropped into the drug underworld. He became a dealer to satisfy his gnawing habit. But it cost him. In 1925, he was lolling in a Terre Haute Haute hotel along with three other members of a "ring." Federal agents slammed into the room and caught the group babysitting $5,000 worth of drugs. Sody went off to Leavenworth for the first time.

Doing hard time did not slake his thirst for narcotics. After his release, Sody fell back into his old world. The feds kept an eye on him and arrested him again for dealing in 1931. Upon his release, he returned to the West End a diminished man, ending up tending bar for Mickey Meharry (who had been sent to Atlanta Penitentiary in 1920 for being a member of the "Terre Haute Dope Ring"). Everyone liked Sody, and he became the popular, garrulous man behind the bar, telling jokes and serving beers.

Still, his past and his habit clung to him. Around Thanksgiving, narcotic agents appeared at the bar and told Meharry they needed to talk to Sody. The Meharrys were afraid their bartender was again bound for prison. Instead, the agents took him to a nearby schoolyard for a little talk. "Listen, Sody," they said, "we know you don't get much out of this, only a little bit [drugs] before and after" making connections for drug deals. So why not help them out with information on the big dealers? It did not work. Returning to the bar, a frustrated Sody sadly told Meharry what happened. "You know what them SOBs wanted? They wanted me to rat on everybody. I'm not gonna do it."

But the feds did not give up. They just came up with a different plan to put the squeeze on Ol' Sody.

Shortly afterward, Sody kept talking about "My girl, my girl." Finally, Maryann Meharry asked him who this girl was he was talking about. He told her it was an older woman who was boarding at Kit Foster's brothel. Meharry was familiar with the woman. She was a gray-haired, very classy-looking woman whose husband was serving time for drug dealing. It didn't make sense to her that the woman was enamored of Sody.

As much as Maryann liked Sody, she did not see him as the answer to a woman's dream. "Sody, get next to yourself. What in the hell would she want with you? I don't mean to insult you or anything, but you lost your eye." He apparently had lost his eye to degenerative eye disease. She pointed out that his only money came from his Spanish-American War pension and what he made tending bar. "She only wants to send you to the penitentiary or get your pension."

As expected, Sody was hurt and angry and left the tavern. He stormed out and headed to a seedy bar on North Third Street. He stayed there three days, sleeping upstairs, before returning to Meharry's. It was then that "his girl" came looking for him.

She told him there were some men outside who wanted to talk with him. They told Sody they were tired of spending money on booze and not getting a big enough kick. They needed an ounce of the good stuff. Sody, who could feel the need for a fix soon, agreed to help and said he would get it and bring it back. "No way," they told him, "where our money goes, we go."

They drove to Webb Berry's place on Spruce Street to make the buy. As soon as the deal was made, the badges came out. His girl had set him up. Maryann Meharry was right. It was another five years for Sody. After his release, the Meharrys took him in, but soon, his health worsened. He went to stay with his older sister in Indianapolis.

He died there in 1936. The cause was listed as acute alcoholism.

MR. HOLLYWOOD

Terre Haute had been the scene of several mobile gun battles between rival bootleggers, one resulting in a killing, over the previous few years. So, in October 1929, when those in the normally quiet neighborhood around Union Hospital heard gunshots, they headed for safety. Those brave enough to peek out their windows saw a scene straight of a gangster movie starring "Shorty" Hollywood.

The next day, a newspaper headline blared, "Gangsters Battle in the Streets." The article featured an exciting account of two cars racing along the street, a Thompson submachine gun spitting bullets from a Chrysler roadster, a wreck and one man chasing another on foot, guns blazing. Breathtaking stuff, alright. But the story, or stories, was a little more prosaic.

The initial story was that Shorty and his wife were driving along Eighth Avenue when he spotted a young man named Walter Blueher driving a yellow roadster turning in front of them. Shorty was not happy with Blueher, whom he felt was paying undue attention to his wife. So, when Shorty saw the young swain, he pulled out his revolver and began shooting at him. His wife was at the wheel and deliberately hit a curb to stop the melee. When Blueher's car had a flat tire at Fourth and Eighth Avenues, he jumped out to run for his life. Hollywood chased him and fired another shot but missed. Hollywood jumped back in his car and told his wife to take off.

Meanwhile, Blueher was allowed into a house to make a phone call. Minutes later, a car with four heavily armed men pulled up and took Blueher away from the scene. Around 2:00 p.m., a woman showed up to claim the car Blueher was driving. She told the police the car was hers. She was a prostitute named Eve Omerad and gave her address as 221 North Third, a brothel. The police took her in for questioning. Shorty went into hiding but was caught in the wee hours of the morning. His story was different than the others.

In his version, the woman driving the car was Omerad (aka Dollie McKay), who was Shorty's love interest, and it was actually Dollie that Blueher was chasing.

Shorty (his draft registration card listed him as five feet, three inches tall and weighing ninety pounds in 1918) was, as they say, well known to the police. Born in Jackson, Michigan, in 1888, he was living in Indianapolis during World War I. He was sentenced to from two to fourteen years in the state prison in 1920. His form does not indicate what crime he committed, but serving up to fourteen years shows that it was serious. Sentences of that length were often meted out for serious assault or intent to murder. One clue might be that he worked as a boilermaker. Metalworkers and boilermakers were in demand during Prohibition as still makers.

Hollywood was released from prison on New Year's Day 1924. Like many others, he eventually made his way to the West End. He set himself up in a houseboat moored under the Wabash River Bridge. It became his floating speakeasy, and he did good business. The boat was known as a "rendezvous for crooks and rum runners." Seven weeks after Shorty's gun battle with Blueher, the police raided the flatboat, arresting Shorty, his wife, Helen, and a "porter" named Woodson.

The police made quite a haul. They seized a large stock of liquor: fourteen pints of bonded whiskey, twenty-five gallons of alcohol, fifteen gallons of wine, two hundred bottles of home-brewed beer and "imitation brandy and crème de menthe." They also found three expensive fur coats they suspected were stolen.

A policeman explained that they had been staking out the houseboat for weeks after getting reports of "high powered cars" with out-of-state plates making daily visits to Hollywood's floating liquor store. Terre Haute was a bootlegger's mecca, and its territory was occasionally fought over by Capone's Chicago mob and a St. Louis syndicate. It seems Shorty was mixing in with the big boys. Hollywood was fined $100 and given a short jail term. No big deal, they were just the costs of doing business.

And business remained good, but Shorty should have cooled it a bit. In March 1930, three drunken high school student were picked up staggering on the street. Their little adventure turned sour when they were hauled to the county jail just yards from Shorty's boat. The clang of a jail cell swiftly melted their shell of teenage bravado. Soon, they singing. They said they had bought pints of liquor for fifty cents from Shorty. They had heard about Shorty from classmates. He had even cajoled them to spread the word to their friends about where they got the booze and that he had plenty in stock.

The police immediately raided the houseboat again. This time, it netted the cops even more large stocks of booze and Shorty another prison term, this time for from one to two years.

By the time of his return, Prohibition was over and bootlegging was no longer a center of profit. Hollywood ended up running a hotel at Fourth and Cherry. His clientele was mostly retirees and prostitutes renting rooms by the hour. He died in 1956.

The Man with Diamond Teeth

Many West End characters could be described as "colorful," but Frank Hess was positively Runyon-esque.

Hess was born in 1876 within what would be the future confines of West End on North Second. It was a hard place to grow up, and he had a series of odd jobs as a youngster. Befitting his birthplace, he was a bartender at several saloons and got involved with the shady dealings and politics of the district. Somewhere along the way, he managed to buy an island. Nine-Mile Island was in the middle of the Wabash River south of Terre Haute. It was a sometime picnicking spot. One group got stranded overnight along the river when the engine on their boat died. The next morning, Hess came to the rescue. He was a temporary hero.

He tried his hand as a boxing promoter in 1914 after prizefights were legalized in Indiana. He became heavily involved in the Donn Roberts machine. He was one of those involved in the illegal voter registration scheme. According to regulations, only his family was allowed to live in his two-story tavern, but somehow, over one hundred people were listed at that address. He claimed that he only did it under threat that he would lose his bar. He compounded this by attempting to bribe fellow Roberts crony Wes Godfrey to flee the state so he would not have to appear as a witness in the federal trial.

The year 1920 was not Hess's favorite. In April, a fellow saloonkeeper named Dobbs, who had previously sold the Hinky Dink, sauntered into the bar with a smile on his face. He told Hess he left some personal items in the bar and wanted to retrieve them. Even though Hess gave them to him, Dobbs turned back and fired four shots. Luckily, Dobbs was no Annie Oakley; one shot killed only a mirror, and the other three grazed the ceiling. Bad aim must have been a Dobbs family trait. The previous day, his wife had taken a shot at Dobbs in their restaurant next door to the Hinky Dink and missed him. It is unknown if the shootings were related.

Hess turned the Hinky Dink into a soft drink parlor. He was arrested for selling booze there in July. Then he was arrested when he was found with a gunnysack full of empty bottles on his way to fill them with raisin whiskey. Then he was fined for having music in the Hinky Dink.

Perhaps to end the year on a positive note, Hess decided to upgrade his appearance. One December day, he sauntered into the office of an accomplished Terre Haute dentist named, appropriately, Dr. Cheek. Hess told him he wanted the best that money could buy. He ordered a gold upper plate with diamonds in the front two teeth. The gold plate was also inscribed with Hess's monogram. The newly sparkling Hess could be seen smiling from a block away on sunny days in the West End.

Hess's new year brought more adventure. He was arrested with a load of raisin whiskey. (Raisin whiskey was a Prohibition attempt at making booze if one did not have access to enough corn syrup or sugar to make real whiskey.) He then decided he needed to buy an airplane, perhaps to smuggle booze from Florida, where Cuban rum was regularly offloaded at sea and sent north. That did not go as well as he hoped. While he was testing the plane, it ventured out to sea and was ditched. Just as Hess had rescued stranded people on the Wabash, he had to be rescued and brought to shore.

He continued to be in and out of trouble. In 1921, he sued a local newspaper for libel. But since truth is the best defense for libel, he lost the case. The next year, he was sentenced to six months in jail for bootlegging. Hess's life went on like that until his death in 1927.

AUDREY DORSEY

Observers that October morning in 1967 saw an older woman scuttle awkwardly into a Terre Haute courtroom. Dressed in a heavy gray coat over a gray suit, she nervously took her seat in the witness chair. She heard her lawyer describe her as a "sick woman racked with arthritis, extreme nervousness and a kidney ailment." She looked wanly at the judge, who was about to pronounce her sentence. The judge looked down at her and softly told her that she was about to be sent to the Indiana Women's Prison for six months for keeping a house of ill fame. It would be her second term there. Though sympathetic to her health, the judge noted that he could "find no legal basis or precedence" to prevent her incarceration.

The graying woman with four grandchildren reached down to steady herself on the witness chair from which she had arisen just a few minutes before. With the pronouncement, a newspaper noted, "a colorful figure [was] removed from Terre Haute's west side." Audrey Dorsey (aka Mary Smith, Clara Jones and Mary Jones), a ubiquitous, ever-moving madam of the West End, was escorted from the room.

Some people break the law, some fight the law. Audrey Dorsey just seemed to ignore it. Dorsey may have been the most arrested madam in the West End. This was partly because of her disregard for authority, and partly because she was Black.

Another St. Louis import, Dorsey appeared in the West End after World War II. Like the majority of Black madams, her houses were on the outskirts of the district, mostly on North Third and Fourth Streets. She was first arrested in 1949, resulting in her first term in state prison. Released in December of that year, she returned to the West End to begin again. It did not take long to make herself acquainted with the police. She was arrested again in 1951 at 105 North Third and fined twenty-five dollars and costs, and again in July 1952, when she and two of her girls were arrested on morals charges. Six years later, two girls "living in her house" were busted for prostitution.

Dorsey once again met the police at the door in 1960. When they tried to take her in, she claimed she was "too sick to appear at headquarters." She did go to court later and received the obligatory small fines. She was arrested again in 1961 along with four of her girls. The girls told police that Dorsey had recruited them to come to Terre Haute because it was "good pickings" in the West End.

Later in the year, she ran afoul of different authorities. This time, it was the taxman. The IRS arrived, looking for Audrey Dorsey (or Mary Smith, Clara Jones or Mary Jones). It seemed Audrey had neglected to pay her taxes. They put a lien on her property of over $14,000. They also came after her son Elmer Young and his wife. Like mother, like son: Elmer had not paid taxes on income stemming from his club, the not-so-appropriately named Jolly Inn, located just south of the West End. The properties were eventually sold for back taxes in 1964.

Elmer had a troubled life with a long string of arrests for intoxication, assault and receiving stolen goods. His club was a trouble spot, with at least one murder arising from a gambling argument in the back room of the bar.

Dorsey was arrested again in 1962 and 1967. Once again, she returned to her old life after release from prison. She was ordered to "close the house immediately" in 1970 instead of paying a large fine. It was her second arrest in three weeks. So she simply opened a new house just outside the West End. She was arrested in 1971 and listed her occupation as "beautician." The house was on North Fourth Street, just beyond Indiana State University. Perhaps that was the last straw, as she later moved to Los Angeles.

THE COWBOY

Frank "Mickey" Meharry was a natural on horseback. He looked good riding on his briskly stepping horse adorned by silver-plated saddle and bridles. Mickey was born in Covington, Indiana, in 1889, although he sometimes gave his birthplace as Jamestown, North Dakota. There might be two reasons for that. For a rodeo man like Mickey, it sounded better to be from North Dakota than from Indiana. Also, his family moved around quite a bit. His brother Lester was indeed born in Jamestown in 1893 and his sister Ruth in Danville, Illinois. Perhaps he simply adopted his brother's birthplace as his own. His brother C.B. "Dude" Meharry later served as sheriff of Stutsman County, North Dakota.

Mickey inhabited two very different worlds: the West End and the rodeo circuit. The West End Mickey was a saloon owner and one-time co-conspirator with ex-brother-in-law and vice king Buster Clark. Abetting Clark's crimes cost him a one-year federal prison term and time in county jails. The rodeo circuit gave him freedom, excitement and friendships with the most important Western movie stars of the day. He spent many summers on the circuit while Maryann stayed in the West End to tend to business. It may have also taken him to Hollywood.

Among his good friends on the circuit were Tom Mix and his wife, Boots Sallie; Ken Maynard; and Tim McCoy. All were huge movie stars in their day. Mickey taught Tex Terry to rope, a skill Terry used in films. Terry was born in Coxville, Indiana, and appeared in over fifty B movies and TV series like *Death Valley Days* and *Bonanza*, usually as a bad guy. Mickey may have served as an extra or a stuntman in several Westerns.

Mickey was a fixture at festivals, parades and sporting events in Terre Haute. He was an impressive sight in his silver-mounted saddle and bridle

Left: Painting of Mickey Meharry by "Salty" Seamon. *Lawson collection.*

Right: Two Meharry girls in front of Mickey Meharry's bar. *Lawson collection.*

and silver-studded chaps. Artist Salty Seamon caught Mickey's spirit in a painting that shows him atop a rearing black horse, white hat, big silver belt buckle and rope in hand. He was also a founding member of the Terre Haute Saddle Club, which had its inception from conversations in his bar.

Mickey and Maryann Meharry were among the couples who formed partnerships in the West End. The husband ran the tavern and the wife the house. Tom and Ruth Brady combined operations at their West End tavern. The bar was on the first floor, with rooms for girls in the back room and upstairs. Jim and Kate Adair had a bar, and the brothel was two doors down the street. The Adairs must have had a tumultuous marriage. Kate filed for divorce at least six times over the years. But they always got back together. Jim always placed a memorial tribute to Kate in the newspapers on the anniversary of her death. George Gillette and his wife had a bar at 121 North Second and a house at 125 North Second. Blackie Write had a saloon across from the farmer's market, while his wife and sister operated a brothel next door. Both places had a rather unsavory reputation.

BAD BLOOD

In the old argument between nature and nurture, whether people are born a certain way or are shaped by their environment, the Jeffers brothers of Taylorville would be a valuable case study.

There seemed be something wrong in their blood that infected all three of them, but they also grew up and lived in arguably the most miserable place in Indiana. Taylorville, on the opposite bank of the Wabash River from Terre Haute, was described as "Sixty Acres of Hell." It was a place that seemed to be made of debris and flotsam, both human and material. It was the place you went to when you had nowhere else to go. The people were wretchedly poor and surrounded by filth and disease.

Taylorville was the home of Joe, Earl and Dean Jeffers—three brothers who suffered the same fate.

Joe Jeffers was indeed a bad man, known as the "King of Taylorville." He was a thug, a gunman and an arm-breaker. Donn Roberts recognized Joe's particular talents early on. He became Roberts's premier strong-arm man. He was an expert at intimidating voters, walking around with his gun out and touting Roberts. More than a few Republicans decided they didn't really need to cast a ballot and walked away from polling places. When the Roberts delegation was refused entry to a Democratic convention in Greencastle, Joe just kicked the door in.

A 1915 drawing of Dean Jeffers, the "King of Taylorville." *Author collection.*

Roberts even named Joe a special policeman in Terre Haute. He was almost never held accountable for beatings. Once when angered by a newspaper story about him, Joe beat a reporter unconscious and then continued kicking him in the head as he lay bleeding on the floor. One reporter was not enough. He then gave the same treatment to the man's colleague.

In 1919, Joe got angry at a man in Taylorville who he felt had mistreated his son. The confrontation led to a gun battle in the street. Joseph McKenzie won the battle. He shot and killed Joe Jeffers. McKenzie was never tried for the killing. Everyone accepted that it was self-defense and secretly applauded the outcome. Just one more bad man off the streets of the West End.

Brother Earl was the next one to go. Earl was a thief and all-around scoundrel. He was arrested in 1916 for "mistreatment of a little girl." He excelled as a holdup man and mugger. He usually got away with it. After all, he was a Jeffers and well protected. His biggest score was in 1920, when he and a partner robbed a man of $1,400. In December of that year, he ran out of luck. Deciding he needed to beat his wife a second time that day, Earl lunged for her. She had finally had a craw full of that bastard Earl Jeffers. She shot and killed Earl with his own gun. Somewhere in the world at that moment, a poet was penning lines about justice.

And then there was Dean Jeffers. Dean appears to have been the most law-abiding, or least law-breaking, of the brothers. He worked in a wagon yard, and his name seldom appeared in court records, though he was undoubtedly a sometime accomplice of his brothers. Oddly, his name twice appeared in the same edition of the *Saturday Spectator*'s week-in-review section. The first announced his marriage to Carrie Jones. Four days later, it noted that Dean had filed for divorce from Jones. No doubt there was an interesting tale involved. Dean's end came in December 1921. He got into a fight with a woman named Margaret Ferguson in a Taylorville saloon. Margaret pulled out a gun and shot Dean to death on the spot.

Three brothers, all shot and killed within two years. The good people of Terre Haute did not mourn them.

THE OTHER, OTHER, OTHER MADAM BROWN

Brown was a popular last name among West End madams.

Ella Brown was a fixture in the "old" West End. She continued her shenanigans in the district after 1906. Ella was a second-generation prostitute-madam whose life was adventurous and violent, to say the least. She was considered quite beautiful and known as the "fair-faced siren." She also appears to have been a fickle young woman.

Ella was the proverbial wild child. Being raised in a brothel, she grew up fast. She liked booze, men and money and wasn't shy about pursuing all three.

She took over her mother's brothel around 1896. Early the next year, a young man nicknamed "Doc" became enamored of the pretty Ella after "visiting" her at her house on North Second Street. A twenty-year-old from a good family, Doc decided that Ella was the only girl in the world for him. After each visit, he asked her to give up the life and marry him. She always demurred, having set her sights on an older, successful man.

Totally besotted with the "Queen of Second Street," Doc tried again on May Day 1897. That Friday, he drew his pay and descended on Brown's house determined to spend it all and make Ella his betrothed. She again turned him down, telling him her heart was set on Peter "Bud" McCoy. Bud was a well-known figure who owned both a successful saloon and a brothel.

Devastated, Doc stumbled through the streets, ending up at Bud's saloon. Somewhere along the way he had acquired a gun. What plans were hatching in his fevered mind? Did he intend to kill his older rival, thus eliminating the roadblock to his joy? Or did he just want to warn McCoy to stay away from Ella?

No matter, Bud was not there. Instead, Doc announced to all and sundry that the great love of his life had spurned him. He had no reason to go on with his life. He might as well end it all. He made a dramatic exit into the saloon's backyard. The boys in the bar just sort of smiled at each other. They were used to such scenes from jilted lovers. They had witnessed them a hundred times. But then a shot rang out in the yard. They rushed outside, only to see Doc just lying there. He missed, he told them. They knew he had probably just shot at the sky. They had a good laugh and went back inside. Did Doc really intend to kill himself? Or did he imagine a romantic scene where word would get back to Ella that he so loved her that he was willing to die rather than live without her, and that she would be so impressed by his devotion that she would marry him? Who knows? Young men sometimes think such things.

The next night, he returned to Ella's, singing his old, sad song. He could not live without her. She again told him she was to marry McCoy, not him. Again, Doc headed to McCoy's place. He sidled up the bar and ordered their cheapest whiskey. He pulled an envelope from his pocket, saying it was filled with powdered morphine, and he poured it into his drink. Having seen this act before, the bartender and saloon loungers laughed when he said his goodbyes to them. Some stood to shake his hand, saying they were sorry his life had come to this but hoped to meet him again someday "in the new Jerusalem."

Doc returned to Brown's house to tell her what he had done. One of the girls sent an emissary to McCoy's to find the envelope. The label said it came from a local pharmacist named Foulkes. A messenger was sent to him seeking an antidote. Foulkes told him not to worry. Seeing the state Doc was in, he had filled the envelope with a headache powder, not morphine. Another bluff called; Doc went on his sad way.

True to her word, Ella Brown went to live with Bud McCoy, though "without the benefit of clergy." Bud was not an easy man to be with, and he never seemed to have much luck keeping wives or girlfriends. Within six months, Ella had her fill of Bud. One day, as usual, she drank too much and stewed over the situation. The best course, she thought, was to leave. She dressed in a man's suit, with a bicycle cap and a light overcoat. Luckily for Ella, the suit had pockets to hold the $800 of Bud's money she took with her.

She headed to her brothel for a while but then "went out to put a few stripes on the city," visiting various saloons and spending lavishly. She then headed for the Big Four train depot, ostensibly to leave town. But, being Ella, she met a man there. Meanwhile, having discovered what was going on, Bud sent the police after Ella and his cash. They swooped in on the depot but missed her. They followed her trail to a local hotel, where they found her and her latest man heating up a room. They took what was left of Bud's money and let her go.

Ella returned to her brothel and took up her old trade. In 1901, she found herself entertaining a client named John McGill in her room. For reasons never explained, she took an intense dislike to McGill. Taking a gun from a drawer, she shot at him but missed. McGill left but did not forget Ella.

Two years later to the day, Ella's drinking and temper got her in trouble again. One night, she sat drinking and "started out to do the levee." She ended up at the Dell Shafer brothel, where she spied Nola McClelland. Nola was another West End character known to be rough as a cob. Brown immediately started shouting vile names at McClelland, who returned her abuse in equally obscene measure. Then the fight began. Nola was an accomplished—and dirty—fighter. She had recently "gouged out the eye of a colored woman with a rusty nail." As they were rolling around on the floor, Nola pulled a knife from her dress. Three quick thrusts pierced Brown's neck and both shoulders. Once again, Nola prevailed, but this time, she feared she had committed murder. She left the house and tried to escape as a doctor tended to Brown's wounds, which he feared might be fatal. Police grabbed Nola as she waited for a train to take her away. Ella survived. Nola sat in jail awaiting trial. She was released when Ella Brown made it known that she would not testify against her friend Nola, and the case was dismissed.

Brown then went to Mattoon, Illinois, for a while. There she found a husband

Terre Haute Daily Tribune readers were shocked to learn that Ella Brown was now Mrs. John McGill! Evidently, McGill could not forget the woman who fired a shot at him two years earlier. The girl with the gun had gotten under his skin. Like young Doc, he had to have her. Whether he followed Ella to Mattoon or was already there is unknown, but there they were married.

It was all just too droll a situation for the *Tribune* writer. "Ella Brown, a well-known woman of the town, promised to hold John McGill's coat while he battled the world for groceries for two." The "intended victim and the would-be murderess are husband and wife." Alas, there was no happy ending to this particular fairy tale. Fickle Ella Brown left McGill to marry West End power John Tierney the next year. That, too, did not last. Ella stayed in Terre Haute until at least 1917, but she then moved to Tulsa, Oklahoma. In 1920, Ella Brown, for "many years a keeper of a pretentious establishment" in the West End, was "mysteriously shot to death" in her home in Tulsa.

5

MADAMS

Successful madams had to have a wide and varied skill set and be many things to the different personalities they dealt with. A madam had to be boss, mother, sister confessor, stern hand to lead and soft shoulder to cry on. But most of all, she had to be a good businessperson. Without that particular skill, her business was all but doomed.

STAFFING

Like any good manager, a madam's most important job was to hire good staff. Maryann Meharry claimed to have had nearly a thousand girls working for her in her forty-five years as a madam. They came from all over, even one from Europe. The girls working in the West End were rarely, if ever, from Terre Haute. It would be too embarrassing for a girl and her client to recognize each other. It was bad for business all the way around, as the customer might shy away from visiting the house again, and it could lead to gossip about both parties.

Surprisingly, good looks were not always a determinant of a successful prostitute. A girl could be "ugly as a scarecrow" and still make a lot of money because of her personality. The ones who could make her clients comfortable were often the most successful and assured she had repeat customers. Still another of Meharry's girls was a joke machine and a great conversationalist. Customers were drawn to her. She made a lot of trips upstairs with men trailing behind her.

In fact, probably the most beautiful girl to work for Meharry almost led to her injury or death. She had a girl who looked just like Marilyn Monroe, right down to her suggestive walk and speech. She attracted the notice of a man who had been haunting the women in Terre Haute. He would identify himself as a federal law enforcement office. On one occasion, he spotted a pregnant woman walking home. He convinced her that he was an officer and said she should not walk home alone. She got in the car, where he raped her.

He was also known to visit West End brothels and flash a badge instead of paying. He entered the Meharry house one evening and was immediately taken with "Marilyn." He became aggressive, and when Meharry tried to intervene, he violently pinned her to the wall. She feared for her life and remembered she had read that if you were going to be shot to turn sideways so the bullet had less chance of slashing though your entire body. "Marilyn" saved her by coming back down the stairs and brushing against the man and disappearing into another part of the house. He turned to go after her but could not find her. Frustrated and fearing he might be caught, he ran out the back door. He was eventually caught when he refused to pay a Black girl and she followed him outside and memorized his license plate number.

Part of a madam's job was to train her girls in the proper way to act and dress. Many were young country girls who were hardly refined. Meharry had one girl who wanted a job but whose manners were atrocious. She would lunge across the table to grab food and use coarse language, so she let her go. She probably moved down the line to a lower-quality house or hooked up with a pimp to work the bars.

The best madams ran a sort of finishing school for prostitutes. In the better houses, like those of Meharry and Edith Brown, the women had to comport themselves as ladies. They weren't to use coarse language or flaunt themselves in front of the clients. Though Madam Brown usually insisted her girls wear evening dress, others were more relaxed. Meharry was less strict with her dress code. Her girls could wear dresses, sheer lingerie and hose or other attire meant to inspire the imagination of men. But whatever they wore, it had to be clean and neat. Their makeup had to be well applied and not make them look like a "painted slut." The girls were required to shower each day before going on the "line."

Tricks of the Trade

Maryann Meharry was very protective of her girls, so over the years, she became adept at "reading" potential customers. She said 90 percent of the men were from out of town, so she seldom dealt with men she knew. She learned to size up a man quickly. An experienced madam could look at a man's clothing and demeanor and tell immediately if they had money. The majority were middle-aged out-of-towners. But West End houses also had regulars from Terre Haute they could count on for steady business. They would be best described as working class. A coal-mining official recalled miners gathering to go "down the line" on payday. The American Can Company was just a block from the district, and groups of its workers would make regular excursions to the houses.

Meharry learned early that young men in their twenties or younger were trouble. They would try to get in without enough money to pay for a "date" and were unruly. She was particularly wary of college students, as officials at Indiana State were always trying to shut down the West End.

Venereal disease and pregnancy were two major concerns in the houses. The girls were taught what to look for—cankers or lesions—when a man stripped down. A man was required to either wash his genital area or let the woman do it. Even then, one could not be sure. That is why Meharry made her girls go to the doctor for a blood test every week. If a john gave them something, they could start treatments immediately. Depending on the era, the girls were required to submit for an STD test at a local clinic or doctor. They were given a "clean certificate" that was posted on the brothel walls to assure clients it was a "clean house." Even some of the regulars that the madam knew and trusted could be a problem. Sometimes, when a girl's regular wanted something a bit different but did not want to hurt her feelings, he would go to another brothel. They just hoped he "didn't bring us something extra," meaning an STD, when he came back.

During most of Meharry's years as a madam, the girls did not use birth control. Condoms were available, of course, but very few men would wear them, as they felt it

Maryann Meharry, circa 1925. *Lawson Collection.*

81

diminished their experience. She recommended the girls use Vaseline for what she thought was its carbolic properties. She followed the old country maxim that "if you grease an egg it won't hatch." Still, some girls did get pregnant. Unlike some madams, Maryann allowed girls with babies to stay in the house, at least for a while. Some went for an abortion, which of course was fraught with danger for women in those days, especially if they went to one doctor who specialized in "five-dollar abortions."

Marketing a brothel could be tricky. Large cities often had "Blue Books." These were published guides to the best brothels in cities like New York, New Orleans and San Francisco. They were regularly updated and purported to be for discerning gentlemen about town looking for respectable establishments. At these brothels, they were assured they would find only the finest young women and the best amenities and did not have to worry about being drugged, dosed (contracting an STD) or robbed.

If Blue Books existed for Terre Haute, they have not survived. West End brothels relied on word of mouth, either by satisfied clients or a few key professionals around town who had ready replies to the age-old query, "Where's a guy find a good time in this town?" This nudge-nudge, wink-wink question was constantly asked of male hotel clerks and railroad porters and, as was known to happen in Terre Haute, even policemen. But the best brothel publicists were usually bartenders and cab drivers. Cabbies were the best source, so much so that some brothels paid a "referral fee" to many drivers for steering customers their way.

"Cabbie" was a young man new to Terre Haute in 1970 when he signed on to drive a taxi. The veteran cabbies showed him the ropes. "Previously, my fellow cabbies had shown me the good cathouses. These were the ones that would pay for customers. I never took a dime. Even as a dope-smoking hippy scumbag [so I was often called] I did not want to be involved in this. Of course, if a fare asked, I took him there for the regular rate and maybe a tip."

Taxi drivers grew used to the strange happenings that took place in their cabs, but Cabbie got a surprise on one of his late-night runs. His dispatcher did not care much for him, so he often gave the worst runs to his young hippy driver. According to Cabbie, the dispatcher:

sent me to the Triangle Bar at 3:00 a.m., hoping I would get knocked off, to pick up a fare at Larrison's Tax service at Fifteenth and Locust. This person was a very respectable appearing Black lady. She was wearing reading glasses on a chain and a nice lady's business suit, like your school principal, maybe. On her lap was an article of red clothing, folded. I was surprised when she had me go to a whorehouse. She was very soft spoken and gave me a good tip, three bucks, I think. There were three houses then that sat in the ell of the paint factory. They were just small bungalows, the backyards were protected by tall chain link fences and I think a Doberman. They had blue porch lights when they were open. Later that night I took a gentleman to this house, I think it was the middle of the three houses. He told me to put the meter on time—six cents per minute and wait for him. When the door opened I was surprised to see my previous fare, she was gotten up like Tina Turner in platform shoes, a huge wig and a tight red hot pants suit open to the navel.

Perhaps his favorite trip involved a bunch of naughty old men. He was called to the Vigo County Home, a nursing home for the indigent previously known as the Poor Farm.

The dispatcher told me to pull up at the back entrance silently—no horn. I did so, and three old guys aged maybe early seventies came out, one was missing an arm, one a leg. They scooted in. Take off, man! When I got to Maple Avenue, I asked, "Who are you guys?" One said, "We are the old soldiers that the dirty bastards have forgot about!" Another said, "I got some money they don't know about and B'gawd we are going to have some fun!" I think those guys were World War I vets, they were about the right age. I took them to a tavern that had food, the Rendezvous, I think. They

Mary Meharry's apartment house-brothel, the "Blue Palace." *Lawson collection.*

paid me and asked me to pick them up in an hour. I promised I would if not on another run. So I did, they were loaded and happy when I got there. "You know where to take us now," one guy said. When I didn't answer, he said, "the cathouse dammit, what kind of a taxi driver are you?" So I dropped them off at the paint factory, because I knew everyone I took there left happy. They called again in an hour. I took them back to the county home. As they got out, a huge female nurse grabbed them and herded them inside. "You boys are in bad trouble," she said. One of them looked back at me and yelled, "It was worth it!" and winked.

Another fare was not as happy with his experience.

Another house of ill fame was the notorious Blue Palace; it sat kitty-corner across Lafayette Avenue from the newly built Lincoln Quad [at Indiana State]. *It was a two-story square apartment house painted robin egg blue.* [It was owned by Maryann Meharry, who loved the color blue.] *It had a balcony with fancy wrought-iron railings like New Orleans. The girls used to stand out there and show off their assets to the college boys. I did not like this place, we had contracts to take the girls to the gyno and give them some time out once a month I think. The women there were not friendly, like the ones from the paint factory block. One time, I took a guy there at his insistence and he left angry.*

Some madams tried a more direct marketing ploy. They were known to gather their girls and take a trip downtown. The first stop was usually the post office, a favorite gathering place of many men. The girls would talk and flirt with potential clients, leaving the heady scent of cologne trailing behind them. Then it was off to do a little shopping. Many male eyes fixed on them as they walked along Wabash Avenue. In the stores, they wound their way through the clothing, possibly pausing in the lingerie department. A slow saunter back to the West End left no doubt where they were to be found.

The best madams also provided good surroundings for the girls with their 50 percent cut of each transaction. The houses were clean. Where down-market houses limited girls to one towel per day and little more than a bowl and pitcher to clean themselves, Meharry and others had clean showers and multiple bathrooms.

Meals were also provided. Meharry allowed the girls to eat any time, provided they do the cooking themselves if they were eating outside regular mealtimes. If not working or sleeping, they were required to eat with the

TERRE HAUTE'S NOTORIOUS RED-LIGHT DISTRICT

family. Edith Brown did have an odd stipulation for her girls. She provided meals, but if her girls wanted dessert, they had to send out for it.

Most madams also paid for the girls' laundry as part of their costs of doing business. This was not always the case. In Al Capone's brothels, the girls were ordered to send their laundry out to a particular cleaner. It was owned by Capone associates, and the girls had to pay several times the going rate to have their clothes washed. It was another way to get more than a fair share of the girls' "cut."

Most good houses had cooks, maids and handymen on staff. They took care of the house and made sure all was tidy. Meharry made sure her girls picked up their own rooms. That was not the job of her cleaning women.

Maryann Meharry tried to foster a "family" atmosphere for her girls. That was simply not the case in most brothels. To many madams, the girls were business assets to be employed until they were no longer of value. However, the brothel system was a much safer environment for girls than working the streets or being controlled by a pimp. There were rare occasions of violence done to girls in brothels, but nothing compared to what prostitutes experienced on the streets.

There is a general understanding of how girls were drawn into the life, but what about madams? For most, it was just a job, a business where they were their own boss for the most part and made good money. Some relished the sheer excitement of it, a tinge of danger, meeting famous people. It was a business to Maryann Meharry. As she said, if she could have gone into another business that paid as much and gave her the freedom of being her own boss, she would have done it.

6

A GIRL'S LIFE

A prostitute has sex for money; a whore does it for free.
—Maryann Meharry

Most people did not care to, or perhaps dare to, look beyond the façade of a prostitute to see the person behind it. It was almost as if they thought there was, apropos of Gertrude Stein's opinion of Oakland, California, "no there there." An article appeared in a 1917 edition of a Fort Wayne newspaper that was rather symbolic of such attitudes. (Fort Wayne newspapers seemed to loathe Terre Haute and regularly published damning articles about the city.)

It reprinted a story from a Terre Haute paper about the efforts to raise money for the Red Cross to aid wounded American soldiers in France. The West End had been generous with its donations. Saloonkeeper Tom Brady started the ball rolling by slapping fifty dollars on his bar and telling the volunteer to wait. He called other saloonkeepers, who arrived to match his donation or give what they had in their pockets. The canvasser was about to leave, surprised to have raised so much money so quickly, when Brady again told him to stay put. "Don't rush off," he said. "Let's see if the girls want to give, too." News spread fast in the West End, and soon, sixty-two madams and girls pushed into the Red Onion saloon to lay their money on the bar. Some did so with a tear in their eye, it was reported.

Instead of seeing it as a nice effort and one that showed that prostitutes were just another part of the community, the writer elevated self-righteousness to an art form. The donations were not done from the heart, he seethed, but for base motives. "Some…outside Terre Haute will see this offering of the depraved denizens of the toughest corner of the Central West as a fine sentiment." Not so, says the writer. "It is well known that gamblers, Cyprians [slang for a prostitute], and other creatures who live by lawlessness maintain a strict regard for business obligations and that they are always generous to charity." They did not do it out of the kindness of their heart. "Goodness is the furthest thing from their perverted minds." They only do it from "low cunning" in a bid for respectability and tolerance.

Prostitution was defined as a "female" crime in Indiana. In essence, legislators were saying that women are directly responsible for the institution of prostitution, not men wanting prostitutes. It is like saying that banks cause bank robbery and thus banks are more culpable than robbers. There were laws that made visiting prostitutes a misdemeanor, but they were almost never enforced. Very few men were ever arrested and charged. If they were taken in, they received fines of just five or ten dollars. Terre Haute newspapers did publish the names of a few men on occasion. Interestingly they never included the names of well-known Hauteans caught in the brothels, unless there was a political advantage to doing so.

Whole forests have been decimated to provide paper for endless and inconclusive discussions about the who, what, when, where and why of prostitution. In modern times, even feminists cannot come to any real agreement. On one side, there are feminists who say that it is a prime example of women as victims. Others see it as women taking some control over their lives and that prostitution is another form of work for women who face the options of other bad jobs. One thing nearly all agree on is that circumstances, none of them good, drive women into the business. No little girl grows up saying that's her dream job.

GOING ON THE LINE

Becoming a prostitute in the West End was called "going on the line." To do so, they had to register with the police. Girls were supposed to register with their real names but seldom ever did. Once registered, they had to go to the health department and be tested for venereal disease and other health issues. If she passed, she was given a certificate that was supposed to be posted in the brothel. She was then required to be tested at weekly or biweekly intervals. If she failed to keep an appointment, she was picked up by the police and taken to the testing site.

Very few girls were drawn to the life after observing higher-class prostitutes from afar. But it did happen. It seemed glamorous to some. Pretty clothes, exciting life, travel, perhaps a good-looking man squiring her around. In modern terms, think of it as the *Pretty Woman* syndrome. You meet and fall in love with a rich, handsome man who understands you and whisks you away to the perfect life. Popular myth was that some women chose prostitution because they were nymphomaniacs and could be paid for doing what they liked best. Obviously, that is a male construct, perhaps to assuage their conscience, or just another way to denigrate women.

That was simply not the case for 99.9 percent of women pulled into the life.

Women did not cross the threshold of a brothel for the first time "undamaged." Most had suffered years of mental and physical abuse. Some were victims of incest or other sexual abuse. They carried those scars, memories and demons with them. Some came from wretchedly poor backgrounds and would do anything to escape that life. Some had fled poorly paid workplaces where they had been continually sexually harassed and figured that if that was going to continue, they may as well be better paid for their efforts. So they adopted new names for a new life.

Maryann Meharry found that she didn't really know the backgrounds of her girls at first. "You never did know where they come from half the time." Only later did some of the truth slip out. "The only time you'd ever get truth out of a girl would be some evening just about sundown." They would sit at a window staring out and begin to reminisce. More truths came out that way than if you asked them directly.

They would "sit there in that rocking chair and rock and just start talking to you, you know, just very nonchalantly telling you the whole works. You'd be surprised how many girls' mother or father come and got their money. How many girls kept their family. How many of 'em had a no-good pimp hangin' on 'em which I could never figure out." Meharry could never understand why some girls "would lay down with a dozen men to give one man your money."

Meharry tried to keep pimps from her girls but wasn't always successful. Some girls "worked" for pimps on their day off. One girl in particular was totally controlled by her pimp. Maryann and her maid noticed that when the girl came to work at the house, she had on the same hat and dress and carried a small suitcase with only a nightgown in it, not even underwear. Meharry couldn't believe it and asked what she would do in case of an accident or something. She told them her pimp wanted it that way. Then it hit Meharry: it was just another means for the pimp to control her.

Pimps became more of a factor during the waning years of the West End. Meharry had to deal with a particularly bad pimp called "Little Bit." He was a member of a notorious motorcycle gang called the Outlaws. Meharry called him the "scum of the earth." By the time her house at 214 Cherry was demolished, she had already set up an operation at her apartment building, the Blue House, on the edge of the ISU campus. One early morning, she walked out on the porch to find a young girl sitting there with a suitcase. When asked who she was and what she wanted, the girl simply said, "I'm gonna work here."

"You are? Who hired you?" The girl nonchalantly told her that Little Bit from the Outlaw gang sent her. That was the first Meharry had ever heard of Little Bit. She soon learned more than she cared to. Little Bit had several girls in the apartments that he was "maneuvering."

Little Bit had a motorcycle and a van he used to "herd the girls around like cattle" to different houses. Meharry had a girl named Billie working for her who kept jumping back and forth from her place to the flat she rented next door to a woman named Rene who ran girls. When told to choose one place or the other, the girl disappeared. A few nights later, Meharry was working in her garden when she saw a motorcycle parked in her yard and a girl scurry out to meet it. Rene came out and said it was Little Bit and Billie. Later Meharry learned that the two had been getting their stories straight. Billie was a wife of an Indianapolis policeman Little Bit had gotten his hooks into. Billie had witnessed Little Bit shoot one of his girls who had stopped working for him.

Some girls were pushed into brothels by their families. That is why relatives came to pick up their pay. Things were so bad at home that the girls were forced to become the family breadwinners. Some were single mothers doing anything they could to support their kids. During the Depression, many women reluctantly took up the life to support the household because their husbands could not find jobs.

Girls did not just shamble into the West End and take up prostitution. First they had to register with the police, who made sure they were not under the age of eighteen. They were supposed to register under their real name, but most didn't. Regulations forbade anyone other than Indiana residents from becoming prostitutes in the state. This meant that many had to lie about where they were from or get someone to vouch for them as Hoosiers. A health test to check for STDs was the final step. After that, they had to report for testing every week, every two weeks or every month, depending on the era.

Girl awaiting customers at Meharry's. *Lawson collection.*

Houses were open twenty-four hours a day and were seldom closed for holidays. Not all the girls actually lived in the houses. They would come in and work shifts, usually twelve hours. In a way, they were contract workers. Those without kids or whose family were far away would become the "holiday girl" so that those with families could take the day off. They were in the house all day and night in case a customer showed up. Customers almost always did, even on Christmas—usually lonely men without family who sought some type of comfort on holidays.

Holidays sometimes led to a surge in daytime business in the West End. Maryann Meharry noticed a pattern, particularly around Christmas and Easter. A car would pull up and park downtown just across from the district. The husband would remind the family how much he hated shopping but did not want to spoil their fun. He would hand his wife some cash and tell her to shop to her heart's content. He might even throw in some extra cash so the wife and kids could have a nice leisurely lunch at a downtown restaurant. "Don't worry about me. I'll just sit here and read the paper or listen to a game on the radio. Maybe I'll grab a beer at a tavern. Go have a good time. No need to hurry."

Soon, the woman and children would emerge from the car and head east on Wabash Avenue. The husband would watch them until they disappeared from view. A few minutes later, he would jump out of the car and head toward the West End to knock on the back door of a house.

There was probably no typical day for a girl working in a house. Again, it depended on the level of the brothel. In the better houses, they rose, bathed and went down to eat. Before their shift, they dressed in their "work clothes." In the better houses, they doffed dresses or gowns. In other houses, it was whatever they thought would catch the eyes of a customer. For some, it was a robe with nothing underneath. For others, it was sexy lingerie, complete with hose and high heels. They dressed to highlight what they thought were their best features. Buxom girls would wear apparel that emphasized their breasts. Those with good legs were liable to wear sheer hose and garters. They would sit with their robe or gown open enough to flaunt their legs.

In the better houses, they would sit in the parlor to greet and chat with clients until they made their choice. Some madams preferred to have the girls make a grand entrance and stand smiling coyly while the man decided which girl was going to be his for the next fifteen minutes. In low-grade houses, the girls were sent to the windows or porch to "rope" in the men. This meant wearing their sexiest, most revealing outfit to attract men. Even worse was being sent into the streets to cajole men into the house. Desperate girls were known to grab men passing by and try to drag them into the brothel.

Their shifts typically lasted ten to twelve hours, depending on volume of business and how many girls were available. The money exchange normally took place in the bedroom. There was no bargaining in the better houses. The fee was the fee, depending on what the man desired. The more he expected, the higher the cost. For girls, the best customers were those who just wanted to be masturbated or who wanted to masturbate while looking at her. The number of men a girl had sex with depended on how busy it was. On a very busy day, girls could average two men per hour. It was not unusual for girls to be with more than twelve men a shift. After each man, the girl would give half of what she made to the madam.

Prostitution was a young woman's game. Their prime years were twenty-one to thirty-one. Not many were still "on the game" after they reached their

Girls "roping" potential customers. *National Archives and Records Administration.*

mid-thirties. It was a maxim among madams that "old girls can't make any money." Girls still working over forty were in a position where they just could not escape the life. Many were alcoholics or addicted to drugs. Meharry had one girl named Nell who was both older and an addict. Nell was her husband's old classmate from Illinois. Meharry knew she was older but told her to come over to stay with her and she would not have to give her a cut. She could keep whatever she made.

There were rumors the girl was an addict, but Meharry did not believe it. She noticed that Nell would have manic surges of energy. She would scrub the walls late at night or launder Meharry's hose. When Maryann told her she didn't have to do that, Nell said she wanted to do it out of appreciation.

One night, Meharry, who lived next door, heard a noise from the brothel. She thought someone was messing with the "plant" at the house. The plant was a device similar to a rolling towel dispenser built into a wall to hide whiskey during prohibition. The next morning, she checked the plant and found that the money hidden there was missing. She watched the girls at breakfast to see if any seemed guilty about something. When all but one girl left, she asked a girl named Helen if she had been in the plant the previous night. She denied it. Angry, Meharry shouted that she would find out who stole it or would fire everyone. Helen decided her job and her son were more important than protecting the new girl and told her it was Nell. It turned out that Nell was indeed an addict. Knowing she could not have needle tracks showing on her body, she shot up under her fingernails. Since she was Mickey Meharry's friend, they did not fire her. Mickey just told her that if another spot opened up at a West End house, she should take it. Nell moved

In the parlor of Mary Meharry's "House." *Lawson collection.*

to a lesser house and was later sent to prison as an addict. Older prostitutes tended to work their way down the rungs of West End houses, even if they were not addicts.

There were girls who were able quit the houses and move on with their lives. A few stayed in Terre Haute. If they encountered an old friend or customer from the house, they tended to react in one of two ways. Some were not ashamed to have lived the life and would stop and talk. Others were so ashamed of their past that they pretended it was a case of mistaken identity and hurried off. Maryann Meharry recalled seeing a girl she knew working as a store clerk. She addressed her by her West End name, and the woman pretended she had no idea who she was. The woman could not get Maryann checked out fast enough. Another time, Maryann said hello to a woman she knew from the district. The first thing the woman whispered was, "O my god. Don't say anything about the West End."

The girls had to be ready for the unexpected. If the customer decided he wanted "extras," she had to deal with that. Sometimes, men wanted more than fifteen minutes or wanted to have another drink first. Good houses like Meharry's had phones in every bedroom so that girls could phone downstairs and relay the requests. Soon, someone was knocking on the door to bring up the drinks or collect the money for extra time.

Of course, there were things no one expected. An older man from Illinois came to Terre Haute to visit a doctor and get a shot. He went to Kate Adair's house in the afternoon. He picked out a girl and she led him upstairs. As he sat on the bed untying his shoes, he gasped and lurched over. The prostitute turned and watched him fall. She shouted for help, and people came running. Someone checked his pulse and said he was dead. Panic set in for a moment, and then it was decided to call the police. Knowing the situation, the police told them to call the undertaker. Someone explained the circumstances to the undertaker. He agreed to tell the wife that her husband suffered a heart attack while sitting in his car and the police brought him straight to the mortuary.

Another man, a politician, was a regular visitor to Moody Jones's place. He came to Terre Haute on New Year's Day. He liked a particular little blonde named Irene who worked there. She was his regular. They were "engaged very busily" when he collapsed on top of her and died. He was a big man, so Irene had a difficult time pushing him off. Irene ran out of the house screaming, scared to death. Ambulances and police came. They took him out of the house and called his wife with the bad news. The newspapers said he died on the street on his way to a football game.

That story is the basis of a piece of West End lore that has been handed down over time. In that version, the man was the mayor of an Illinois city. When he died, the madam called the Terre Haute mayor, who told her to get him dressed and take him to a dark corner of the Schultz

Girl awaiting customers at Meharry's. *Lawson collection.*

95

Department Store parking lot. When his wife came to identify his body, she asked why he was perfectly attired but not wearing socks!

Many girls married and had happy lives after leaving the scene. Sometimes, their husbands knew of their past; sometimes, they did not. It did not surprise Meharry that girls made good wives. Many were good cooks and housekeepers and certainly knew about the vagaries of men.

Much rarer was a girl marrying one of her clients. Longtime Terre Haute resident Joe Walker knew of one case. He knew a woman who "spent part of her life as a prostitute down on the West End." She had a regular customer who visited her almost every week. He was just an ordinary guy. He was very shy and almost never dated. He became very infatuated with the girl and one day asked her to marry him. She told him she would not marry him in Terre Haute but would do so "someplace else." They moved to Indianapolis and got married. It was by all accounts a good marriage.

That man was an example of those who did not go to brothels strictly for sex. He was a lonely guy who perhaps wanted to feel a sense of intimacy along with sex. There were many men who went to the houses but seldom went upstairs with a girl. They were just as happy to sit, have a beer and chat, to feel part of something. Some madams would not stand for that, but others thought it was fine, as they were making good money off the overpriced drinks they sold.

Though the girls were often judged on their looks, they had almost no choice when it came to the men who wanted them. It was pretty much come one, come all. Their clients were seldom wealthy, good-looking men about town. Most were middle-age and looked it; balding, chubby, anxious men who sought release. Many men visited a brothel because it was the only place they could have sex. Some were disabled, scarred, too old or had something about them that made them unattractive to women. There was no place else to go to satisfy their needs.

Maryann Meharry had several girls who stayed almost ten years with her, off and on. Girls were always leaving and coming back. One girl was with her for over ten years but would come and go. She would be with her for a while and then say, "Well, I'm going up to Muncie and stay with Em and Chip for a while." Then, a few months later, she would come back, only to leave again. Sometimes that solved a problem for madams. Girls could get "old on the job," become "stale" after a while. Customers got tired of seeing the same old faces and would go to another house. It was just part of the business. Meharry understood it, as long as the girl did not just sneak off. Her feeling was, "Come in like a lady and leave like a lady."

There was life after prostitution. Though the girls were unaware of the modern term *transferable skills*, they did have them. Their skills were perfect for the business or sales fields. Successful prostitutes were good judges of character, and they had to communicate and sell themselves to clients. In essence, they were expert marketers. If they could market themselves, they could market other goods. They were risk-takers, not afraid to take chances. They were competitive. Some took these skills into jobs like retail sales. Many residents in Terre Haute never had a clue that the woman on the other side of the counter had started out as a prostitute.

Maryann's daughter thought that was one of the things her mother tried to teach her girls. She knew that the girls had little longevity in the "life." Meharry wanted to show the girls "how to be a lady and think better of themselves" as they moved forward.

7

REVIVAL AND DECLINE

1946–61

With the end of the war, the West End started to revive. Houses began to reopen, and activity picked up. A major change was that Edith Brown had closed her house in 1942. Well, not completely closed. She turned it into a "rooming house for men." At one point, she called local newspapers to ask irately why her ad for roomers had been dropped. The young man, recognizing the address, told her she had to call back the next morning, as he did not know the answer. The next day, he told a lady in circulation about the call and asked what was going on. She told him the address was too well known and that the paper would be a laughingstock if it printed the ad.

Another change was in the atmosphere in the district. It was safer and less raucous than in previous decades. The days of gunfights in the streets, killings and drunken brawls involving scores of men and women were gone. With Prohibition long over, bootleggers and gangsters no longer thronged the streets. There was still trouble on occasion. A few small fights broke out, but murders did not occur on a regular basis. Visitors did not have to be as wary on the streets thinking muggers could spring on them at any time. Gambling was not the major draw it had been in the district. There were still a few card and dice games in the tavern, but the big-time gamblers had moved to roadhouses, into clubs like the Idaho Club south of downtown or into bars and joints along Wabash Avenue, as would be subsequently revealed by national magazines.

All in all, this was a kinder, gentler version of the West End.

Ralph Tucker throwing out the first pitch at a Terre Haute Phillies game. *Author collection.*

The year 1948 brought a new man into the mayor's office. Ralph Tucker was a likeable, charismatic person. A newspaper editorial published before the election tasked voters with taking notice that the two candidates' platforms both promised progress for the city. However, it said Tucker's idea of progress was different. After talking to some of Tucker's "henchmen," the editor decided that his idea of progress was "wide-open gambling and restoration of the red-light district.

Tucker did have a pragmatic view of vice, one that was perfect for the West End. Like many before and after him, he saw prostitution as a fact of life, a necessary evil. The best that could be done was to restrict it to one area and maintain order within its bounds. Thus, he had no real desire to meddle in the red-light district.

The new mayor grew up in poverty and spent much of his life in orphanages. He had an engaging personality that took him from salesman to radio personality to the mayor's office. He was "colorful" and had strong views about the powers of a mayor and the political machine's right to rule. In this he was much like Chicago mayor Richard Dailey, whose twenty-year tenure in office paralleled that of Tucker's (1948–68).

He viewed gambling much the same way. As long as it was in private and done willingly, it should be left alone. Tucker liked to play cards and bet on the horses. He was also quick on his feet. Once, while placing a bet in a downtown bookie joint, he was utterly surprised when the place was raided by the state police, who rushed into the back room to arrest the gamblers. The mayor being arrested in a bookie joint while placing a bet would have done no good for his political career or the reputation of Terre Haute. Tucker briskly stepped forward, announced he was the mayor, and said that he had been waiting there to help the police mop up the gamblers. He then ordered the bookies and fellow gamblers to line up and give the police their names.

Though Tucker's Democratic regime was known to take money from brothel owners and gamblers, he was generally portrayed as a man who did not personally take bribes. Maryann Meharry insisted that she never gave protection money to Tucker or any other mayor. Noted historian Edward Spann, in his biography of Tucker, wrote about the rumors of payoffs, but noted that the estate Tucker left to his family was not that of a wealthy man.

However, three of his police bodyguards told different stories. A Terre Haute police detective said that he would drive Tucker around the West End on Saturdays. While Tucker sat in the car, the detective would go to see the madam with a deck of cards in his hand. They would draw for high card, the winner getting the agreed-on sum of money. It seemed Tucker never lost a hand. Still another bodyguard recalled driving him to the West End. A third would take him and recalled sitting in Eddie Gosnell's Rod and Gun Club, which featured gambling, while Tucker and Gosnell met in another room.

Grocery store employee Dick Falls recalled a Saturday when he carried Tucker's purchases out to the parking lot and deposited the bags in Tucker's trademark Thunderbird convertible. As he did so, madam Nell Bundy pulled up next to Tucker. As Falls was walking away, he saw Tucker get in her car and pull away. The next time he went out, Tucker's car and groceries were still there. An hour later, Falls noticed the car was gone.

Did Tucker accept personal bribes? It cannot be said for certain. He may have been taking it to finance his political machine. Like most ardent gamblers, he lost more than he won. Maybe he was arranging for gambling debts to be wiped off the book. But, as Spann noted in his book, Tucker did not die a wealthy man.

Tucker did visit the West End. One morning about 6:00 a.m., two men showed up at Maryann Meharry's back door. It was a great time at the house, "'cause everybody's having a good time and money's rolling in." She couldn't quite make them out due to shadows. She asked if they were coming in, and they hesitated. Another customer was waiting to get in behind, and they stepped aside to let him in. She then recognized Ralph Tucker and his police chief, Carl Riddle.

Tucker asked if she was going to serve breakfast, and she said she didn't know. An upset Tucker growled, "You empty this house up. You got more people here than there is at Seventh and Wabash." Meharry was hard to rattle. She told them there was more to do at her house than at Seventh and Wabash and went back into the house.

The party continued. Meharry told her guests that Tucker wanted her to close up and send everybody home. A chorus of "To hell with him" greeted her. When she kiddingly said he might make her pay for not closing up, a voice from the back yelled, "To hell with him. He better not." Meharry figured nothing would happen. Among the chorus hooting at Tucker was a U.S. House of Representatives member from northern Indiana. His car and others with government license plates were parked outside her house. It is likely a patrolman spotted the plates and reported it to Riddle, who got Tucker out of bed. For his part, Tucker was probably trying to prevent an embarrassing situation if the representative was caught in the house.

The Not-So-Grand Jury

On October 29, 1958, a Terre Haute police patrolman spoke to a forum for prosecutor candidates organized by local church leaders. What he told them led to a special grand jury investigation into vice in Terre Haute. Officer Jack Lowder shocked the group by claiming vice was getting out of control and that city officials didn't care. He said truckers and visitors routinely asked him where to find brothels and gambling dens. On one shift, he said he counted fourteen brothels working full-tilt. Even worse, when he "arrested customers of the houses," they were never charged for the crime. They were set free. He did not say if he arrested any madams or girls.

The next day, Mayor Tucker, Police Chief Carl Riddle and three police captains were summoned to appear before the jury. Tucker was outraged and said Lowder had gone too far when he arrested an eighteen-year-old boy trying to enter a brothel. He should have given the boy a scare and simply warned him and let him go. What good would it do to charge the boy and expose his name in a trial? It would just ruin his life. Lowder was immediately transferred out of the West End. When Tucker was asked by a reporter about Lowder, he told him that "I've been too lenient with the police. We must have more discipline."

Four madams, Dovie Jones (aka Lovie Wells), Nelly "Jew" Bandy, Audrey Dorsey and Meharry, were also summoned.

The next day, it was announced by the judge that the grand jury probe would be delayed until after the election. The reason given was "a desire to avoid any political implications." What he meant was that any buzz about the grand jury would only hurt Tucker's Democratic Party in the election. The Democrats retained control.

Three ministers and a church woman asked to meet with the mayor. During the thirty-minute conversation, Tucker told them that even "the Bible says there will always be prostitution." He also averred that he had been misquoted about dismissing Lowder, even though he also said he had not yet read the newspaper in which the quote appeared.

Two days after the election, the jury foreman, future legendary Indiana newsman Howard Caldwell, asked to have the grand jury reconvened the following Monday. It reconvened the following Wednesday. In addition to those called earlier, madam Betty Doty was also summoned. At the end of the day, the court issued bench warrants for six people who had failed to appear as ordered, including Maryann Meharry, Rose Moon and Kate Adair.

The probe ended on Friday with four indictments, three for prostitution against Charles and Rose Moon and Thelma Booker and one for attempted bribery of the mayor. Walter Guess had offered Tucker money to allow him to open a brothel and exempt him from possible prosecution.

The official jury report stated that there was "no major prostitution or gambling" in Terre Haute. The difficulty with gambling, it said in a disingenuous statement, was "trying to draw the line" on what levels of gambling to prosecute. After all, churches, charities and fraternal organizations all had fundraising events that could be called gambling.

There were immediate cries that the grand jury was merely a show, a sham. It was a "whitewash of the entire vice system" in the city. And, of course, it was. A grand jury can only decide to press forward based on the evidence and witnesses. None of the witnesses had pled the Fifth Amendment, so it seems that if they were pressed harder, they would tell all. It seems likely that a political arrangement was made to brush it under the rug and not embarrass anyone or any party. The fact that Ralph Tucker and some of his cronies had an affinity for gambling perhaps explains why so little attention was paid to that particular vice.

Communities

The West End had two separate but interlocking communities. There was the community within the houses and that of the people who lived within its boundaries but were not connected with the business. Many would be surprised how well they lived alongside each other. As the number of houses devoted to prostitution shrank over the years, average families moved into them. They knew what they were moving into.

Photographer Kenneth Martin was extremely familiar with all areas in Terre Haute. He felt the West End of the 1940s and '50s looked like a very "respectable" area, just like any other residential neighborhood. Except, of course, that some houses were used "for other than normal purposes." As a teenager, Martin hauled produce from area farms to the farmer's market. One of the ways he could differentiate between the brothels and homes was the windows. Brothels always had their drapes open with girls sitting in the windows

On a dare from a friend, he ventured into a house while his truck was being unloaded. As he hesitantly stepped into the empty living room, a girl came down the stairs. She was tall, pretty and wearing a nice black dress. She softly said, "Kid, beat it. You got no business here." Martin was gone in a flash.

Bob Kadel, an award-winning, globetrotting photographer, felt much the same way. He went to school with Nell Bandy's brother Max. He thought they were "good people," much like other families. Kadel was warned to stay away from the West End by his parents but realized later that West End folks were much like everyone else. He figured they had a "life to live too." It was just different than most.

Paul Nasser's extended family owned grocery stores and other businesses in the district. He noted that he always felt safe there. They paid their bills and lived their lives. He was very appreciative that the madams and girls were "very, very liberal" with their donations to his beloved boys club.

The West End was not surrounded by ten-foot walls topped by barbed wire. There were no guards in sentry boxes checking papers. Though some on the outside might not acknowledge it was so, the madams and girls felt themselves part of the larger community. They supported each other in bad times but also were swift in joining in citywide efforts and charities.

West Enders subscribed to the "taking care of your own" ethic. Though there was sometimes fierce competition between the houses, the girls could also come together, as in the case with Jimmy Dorris.

Meharry House at 214 Cherry. The building to the left was the Meharry family home. *Lawson collection.*

Dorris was a West End hanger-on who fell down the steps of a bootlegging joint on Fourth Street. He was initially taken to jail but had to be transferred to the hospital. Maryann Meharry checked on him with a nurse she knew and was told that he was "critically critical." The nurse was reluctant to give her any more information, but Meharry told the nurse that Jimmy didn't have any family. She wanted to make sure he was taken care of properly if he died. Maryann immediately canvassed the neighborhood and collected money to help bury Dorris. Another madam had an extra plot at Woodlawn Cemetery that she donated. She also had a suit to bury him in. Jimmy Dorris was given a respectable funeral by the West End.

A sense of family was very important to Meharry. She and Mickey had two adopted daughters and fostered several other children over the years. For many years, their family home was located next to the house. Their children interacted with the girls, including having breakfast at the brothel. They were restricted to only the kitchen. The rest of the house was off limits. Meharry tried to incorporate that sense among her "girls." They ate with the family and shared activities. "We lived like a large family," Meharry said.

She would often sit in the evening with the girls. As Meharry loved music, they would gather around her piano and sing. She had one girl who played saxophone, another violin. Knitting, sewing and crocheting were also shared activities in the house. Some girls made their own clothes. Meharry once

Gathering of Maryann Meharry and her girls. *Lawson collection.*

bought a bundle of dresses from Goodwill for the wool. They reduced the dresses to carpet rags. She, the girls and even some customers sewed them into braided rugs. Three of the rugs were installed at the Paul Dresser Home historic site. In the middle of one sewing session, a girl named Peg looked up and exclaimed, "You know, this is not a whorehouse; This is a goddam girls' school. All we ever do is work!"

Meharry's house was filled with more than one thousand books. She loved historical novels and books about Ireland. She was also a fan of nineteenth-century French novelist Eugene Sue. A former surgeon in the French army and a contemporary of Charles Dickens, Sue also wrote serialized novels whose most memorable line was translated into English as "revenge is a dish best served cold." One favorite pastime was an example of how many girls came to view the madam as a mother figure. The girls often asked her to read to them. Of course, these homey evenings were often interrupted by customers knocking on the door.

Few madams treated girls like family as Meharry did. To many, girls were simply employees, and the harder they worked, the more the madam made. After all, it was a business.

Maryann Meharry's love of books and antiques led to a friendship with a customer who was the most celebrated novelist in America at the time, James Jones. His masterful novel about the peacetime army, *From Here to Eternity*, had caused a sensation. The novel's frankness shocked many, and Jones's rough-hewn, pugnacious characters fascinated even those who thought the work was obscene. When the book was turned into an award-winning movie with Burt Lancaster, Montgomery Clift and Frank Sinatra, his stature only grew.

Jones, born and raised in Robinson, Illinois, was already familiar with Terre Haute before he wrote the book. Robinson was only about fifty miles from Terre Haute, and Jones began his visits to the city as a teenager. In fact, he may have contracted his first case of venereal disease in a Terre Haute brothel when he was only eighteen.

He joined the army the next year and was stationed in Hawaii in 1939. There he was a regular visitor to the Honolulu brothels catering to servicemen. His frank descriptions of those visits were among the most shocking aspects of his later book. James Jones knew brothels.

In 1951, Jones became a founding member, along with Lowney Handy and her husband, of the Handy Writers Colony in Marshall, Illinois. The colony's guiding force was Lowney Handy (who was also Jones's lover), who tried to maintain an ascetic atmosphere. She expected her writers to maintain a strict schedule, which included them copying the books of an author they admired (her peculiar theory about how to teach writing), then move on to their own books. They also were required to help with construction of the colony and perform other chores.

Lowney Handy did not allow the writers' girlfriends at the colony, because she thought it distracted them. But Handy also knew her varied group of young men needed to occasionally blow off some steam. They were allowed to leave the colony on certain weekends, and many of them raced the twenty miles to Terre Haute bars and brothels. Kenny Snedeker, a member of the colony, noted that "some of the fellows could go to Terre Haute to the whorehouses, if you had the money, which I never did." Jones would roar off on his motorcycle or his Buick to raise his own particular brand of hell in the West End. He explored Terre Haute, drinking in the town, as novelists do. His preferred drinking spot was Bohannon's on Wabash Avenue, where he would chat with the other drinkers and listen to their stories. Who knew where or when something piqued his interest and would make it into his next novel?

Jones was an almost weekly visitor to Meharry's, and they became friends. They shared a love of books and antiques, and several times Jones tried to buy some of her collection. Jones was not always a "bed customer." He loved to sit in the book-lined parlor and just drink Coke and chat with her or the girls. It seemed to relax him.

Meharry thought he was a down-to-earth guy. However, she did notice that after one of his trips to Hollywood for the filming of *From Here to Eternity*, he began to "affect those tennis shoes and little tight (I call 'em jelly bean pants) you know, jeans." Jones told her she should read his new book, as she or her house might be in it. In one of his books, he did mention the library she kept in her room.

John Bowers, another "student" at the Handy Colony, left a vivid description of one trip to Terre Haute in his book titled (appropriately enough) *The Colony*. It was the custom of the veteran writers to initiate newcomers into the delights of a trip to Terre Haute. This particular time, Bowers and the others started out at the Marine Room bar at the Terre Haute House. After a few drinks at this upscale watering hole, they moved to a "subterranean working class bar" along Wabash Avenue. Fortifying themselves with a few more—and cheaper—drinks, they headed to the West End.

Cover of the novel *The Colony*, about the Handy Writers' Colony. In included a chapter about visiting a West End brothel. Drawing of James Jones and Lowney Handy *(foreground). Author collection.*

They ended up at a brothel on Cherry Street. They went to the back door, which was so sturdy that it would have been easier for the group to force its way into a bank than the cathouse. Pushing the buzzer, the men were met by a short, thin, unattractive women. She eyed them expertly to see if they should be allowed entry. Finally, she recognized one of the group, saying, "I remember you." They were invited in.

They were first shown into a large bathroom before being allowed into the parlor, which

Meharry girls had class, circa 1953. *Lawson collection.*

Bowers thought looked like a doctor's office, complete with old magazines should they want to read while awaiting their appointment. The girls emerged from behind a doorway. On offer were four prospective temporary partners. The first was a "well-built brunette in a peek-a-boo harem outfit," looking for all the world like a desert princess awaiting her handsome sheik.

Next to her was a weary-looking older woman whose face told the story of her years as a prostitute. She was wearing a slit skirt and very high heels. Next was a redhead wearing a revealing silk bathrobe. Finally, there was a pretty young blond with a bow in her hair.

The hard-looking woman asked if they were boys just off the farm looking for a little fun. One of the Bowers group told the women they were from the writer's colony and were friends of Jim Jones. The older woman said she had heard of it and liked Jones's book. "What was it, the…Naked and something or other?" She had confused Jones with Norman Mailer and his book *The Naked and the Dead*. They politely refrained from telling her she was talking about Mailer's book, not Jim's. No sense in upsetting a potential good bed partner.

The older woman brushed her hair back in what she must have assumed was a seductive way and started the real proceedings by asking, "Who wants a date?"

Bowers quickly chose the quiet blond, who led him to a room. The room was clean, with a linoleum floor and a much-used pink bedspread covering a narrow bed. She stripped down to just her panties and bra. He handed her the five-dollar fee. The blond dipped a washcloth into a bowl of sudsy water on the bedside table. She washed his genitals in a very impersonal, clinical manner, as if she were a nurse giving a sponge bath to a patient.

She lounged on the bed, one leg cocked provocatively. She asked him how he wanted it. Bowers was not yet experienced enough to know to ask for a "half and half," which was both oral and vaginal sex. Instead, he said he would like the usual. She smiled, knowing she would only have to do half the work for her fee. She removed her underwear and lay flat on her back and parted her legs. Bowers pulled an ancient condom from his wallet. She insisted she was clean and not to worry about protection, but he insisted. She just gave him a look.

Bowers climbed on top of her. It was rather impersonal, he thought, as if he were in some way detached from his thrusting body. He suddenly asked where she was from and learned she was a fellow Tennessean. When he asked the inevitable question about how she got in the game, she said simply that she sort of fell into it. Tired of the chatter, the blond tersely asked if he was "going to come or take all night?" Time was money in her line of work.

As soon as Bowers orgasmed, she was out of the bed in a flash. She washed herself and dressed again, leading him back to the parlor. The others in his group had already finished and were sitting back with smarmy grins on their satisfied faces. Not wanting the night to be over just yet, they went to another bar, ate shrimp and drank beer before leaving Terre Haute.

All in all, their experience in the West End was pretty typical of that shared by thousands of others over time.

The madam did take issue with some of what Bowers wrote. She was unhappy with his depiction of the brothel. She knew the house it was based on. It was one operated by her friend Rose Moon. She felt that it made Moon's place look tawdry, particularly his description of the worn bedspread. Rose always kept a clean and neat house. But, as she noted, those

Relaxing. *Lawson Collection.*

writing about brothels usually depicted them as tawdry. "That's where their taste took them, but it wasn't really the norm."

Jones began work on *Some Came Running* while at the colony. His Terre Haute visits helped shape the novel. All those sites, people and events stayed in his mind. In some ways, Terre Haute was a character in the book. Several scenes took place there, as when the main characters went gambling in the Twelve Points area, where Eddie Gosnell had several gambling operations. Jones "transplanted" a Terre Haute bar called the Health Office to his fictional Parkman, Illinois, taking both the name and description of the place.

Terre Haute is mentioned over forty times. Perhaps the key to how Jones viewed the city is the way he presents some Terre Hauteans. This is particularly evident when he has women from the city make appearances in Parkman, often as girlfriends of characters in the book. They are usually described as pushy, brassy, rather hard women. They were portrayed as drunken, grasping sluts. Such were Jones's versions of Terre Haute. But maybe that's where his taste took him.

Maryann Meharry was heavily involved in community groups and charities. She was the West End captain for the Community Chest charity. One year, she could not lead the fundraising campaign because she and Mickey were visiting his family in North Dakota. Instead, a "Major" in the Volunteers of America was assigned the West End. When Meharry returned, she got a call that the campaign hadn't been completed and was asked to finish it.

She immediately contacted the major to see what was left to do. The major hemmed and hawed but finally mumbled that he hadn't canvassed the West End because there were places Meharry could go but he couldn't. Though she knew the answer, she pressed him about what places those were. "You know them places," he stammered. "Places with girls?," she asked.

A 1955 aerial photo showing the West End, by Robert Kadel. *Kent Kadel collection.*

"Yes." Maryann knew it was a classic case of, "Their money is good, but not them." He admitted that he just didn't want to deal with them. An angry Meharry returned to the West End and knocked on every door. Her message to the other madams was simple. Your money is good, but not you. She asked them not to give money to the Community Chest again. Instead, they should give it to another charity who did seem to think them unclean.

Meharry and other West Enders dealt with such rank human hypocrisy every day. When asked about local churches and groups that looked down on them, she had a ready answer. "Ooh, yes! They were always down [on us] 'til they had tickets to sell for suppers or something. That's [the West End] the first place they went to sell the tickets. Churches, or hospitals, the police ball. Hell, everybody come selling you something. Any other time, you wasn't no good."

There was another "good Christian" she distinctly remembered, a "Brother" at a local church. "I had the back end of the tavern rented to this Sylvia I talked about. I went back there to tell her something one day, and here's old Brother —— with his arms around her, and I thought he was an octopus. What the hell are you doing with *him* in here? 'Oh, he is a friend of mine, ain'tcha, Honey?' I said, 'He is?' 'Shure, he comes to see me every Monday.' I said, 'That explains it. He gets the money Sunday out of the collection plate, I guess.'" Meharry then told her that her friend had a little sideline going. He walked the West End, trying to get a girl to "rope" him. "Roping" referred to a girl sitting in a window and beckoning a customer to enter the house. This method was frowned on by authorities. Then he would write the address in a little book and report it to police.

Perhaps Meharry's most frightening experience came not in the days of gangsters and Prohibition, but during the Christmas season in 1955. It all began in Bloomington, where two Indiana University students, both described as "above average students," robbed a dry-goods store around 2:00 am. Richard Lewis broke into the store and carried out thirteen guns and fourteen boxes of ammunition, while Richard Adams served as the lookout. So what to do after you've stolen thirteen guns? May as well use them. Lewis was from Terre Haute, where his father was an attorney. He knew places that would still be open. And because of their business, they might not even report a crime if they thought it might bring them problems.

The two robbers then headed up State Road 46 on the two-hour drive to the West End. Parking on Cherry Street, they knocked on the back door of Meharry's brothel. She answered to two young men sticking a .45 pistol and a shotgun in her face. She knew the best thing to do was give them money and hope they went away. They did. She called the police, and the holdup boys were arrested with the guns, ammo and forty dollars from Meharry. Meharry identified them, and they immediately confessed to their crime spree. Adams was given a suspended two-to-five-year sentence. Tragically, Lewis committed suicide in May 1956 when police "surprised him in the basement of a Terre Haute American Legion post."

IT'S NOT ALL VICE

There was more to the West End than brothels and bars. Five grocery stores served the district in the 1950s. There was a drugstore behind the Indois Hotel just a block away. Two businesses brought people into the West End on an almost daily basis: the Farmers' Market and Furr's Fish Market. There were also two "hotels," a car dealership and warehouses. There were charity missions. For many years, there was an elementary school, not to mention all the family homes throughout the district. There were no churches.

NICE DOING BUSINESS WITH YOU

The West End brought a lot of money into Terre Haute. In modern terms, it was a sex tourism site. All those out-of-towners who brought their wallets and desires into the district filled more than a few coffers in Terre Haute. The biggest beneficiaries were the downtown retailers, but many other businesses also got their share. The equivalent of many modern millions of dollars changed hands every year.

Brothels and prostitutes were good customers, and they usually paid in cash. The houses needed to be furnished, and that meant sales for furniture and department stores. Chairs, sofas, lighting fixtures, coffee tables, bedside tables and, of course, many, many beds were needed. These were purchased in downtown Terre Haute. Even if some brothels did not change sheets after each "use," vast amounts of linens were needed. Most brothels did their own laundry, but others filled the baskets of dry cleaners and laundries. Food was purchased from local groceries, many of which made daily deliveries in the West End. Coal bins and oil tanks had to be fille for heating.

But it was the money spent by madams and their staff that were a boon to downtown Terre Haute merchants. As their income was higher than that of most women of the area, a visit from West End women filled many a cash register. They bought jewelry, furs, cars and many, many clothes. The madams felt that the closing of the brothels in the 1960s and '70s was a major factor in the decline of downtown Terre Haute. As late as 1965, an Indianapolis newspaper figured the West End was generating $1 million in profit—not total dollars, but net proceeds.

Sid Levin, who owned a furniture store until the late 1960s, thought the West End was very good for businesses. The houses paid their bills on time and, even better, paid in cash. To him, they were to be respected like any other customer who walked through the doors. Other furniture store owners agreed. Madams bought a lot of beds, mattresses, chests and other furniture over the years. And most of them bought quality merchandise.

The brothel staff did not always have to go shopping to get what they needed. Future mayor Leland Larrison's family owned a drugstore. As a teenager, he would make two trips a week delivering cosmetics to fifteen or twenty brothels. While the average person could only afford to spend two dollars or so a week at the store, the West End women would spend ten to fifteen dollars a week or more. Those purchases did a lot for the store's bottom line, especially during the Depression.

Both madams and girls shopped at downtown stores. Clothing stores, jewelry shops and department stores loved their business, even if some owners and clerks looked down on them. The West End helped put food on a lot of tables in Terre Haute, paid for a lot of cars and put many kids through school.

The person who was the West End to many people, the legendary madam Edith Brown, died in 1956. In the early 1950s, she sold her house to Maryann Meharry, who resold it a year later. Edith moved to Sarasota, Florida where she passed on at age seventy-four.

8

THE LONG GOODBYE

1962–72

As the 1960s started to settle in, many Americans thought the country was entering a new age. There was a charismatic, youthful president; the economy was doing well; and a space age seemed just on the horizon. Americans saw many fine changes ahead. Those on the West End saw only a murky future.

The new decade would be the beginning of the end for the district. Two enemies—one new; another an old, implacable foe—were gathering against them. Added to them was a third, even more dangerous enemy, one that could not be defeated. Time and change always won.

The first blow was struck by the *Saturday Evening Post* on February 2, 1961. "Indiana's Delinquent City" was written by respected journalist and editor Peter Wyden. Once again, gambling and prostitution were the foci of the article. On his first day in town, Wyden came upon a roulette wheel in a club on Wabash Avenue. A few steps more took him to a bookie joint. There was no shortage of gambling joints in Terre Haute.

When Wyden asked Mayor Tucker about gambling, he was assured it was all small-time and private. Tucker offered up an interesting metaphor to explain it. It's like "a woman walking around nude in her home without shades drawn. You could arrest her for public indecency," he explained. But what good would that do?

And then there was the West End. Wyden noted that Terre Haute's red-light district was "one of a...dozen communities in the nation with a 'line'—well-defined red light district." Of course, prostitution was found in other areas of the city, but the West End was still the center. Some residents matter-of-factly told him that there were only about a dozen brothels in town, as though that was a perfectly acceptable number. No big deal.

He searched for answers as to why Terre Haute was as it was. He interviewed local community leaders like John Lamb, head of the Chamber of Commerce, and others. They complained that the city was backward. There was no sewage treatment plant, no civic auditorium and no public swimming pools. People didn't give a "hoot." Lamb deplored the deteriorating buildings and dirty streets. It was all due to a lack of will and effective leadership.

The *Saturday Evening Post* article was a gut punch to Terre Haute. Many civic leaders fell back into the usual mantra, "it's not that bad." Everything that was written was "sensationalized." They are always picking on poor old Terre Haute. But a group of housewives decided something had to be done. And if the men who ran the city were just going along as before, then they would have to take on the task of bettering Terre Haute.

The article was the last straw for four women: Jacqueline Becker, Jane Hazledine, Elvira Carle and Joan Marx. Less than two weeks after the article appeared, the women announced the formation of group to seek progressive change in backward Terre Haute. They called themselves the Housewife's Effort for Local Progress, or HELP. The movement took off immediately. They set up an office downtown on Wabash Avenue. Within a month, more than one thousand people had joined the group.

They published an open letter to Peter Wyden, author of the *Saturday Evening Post* article. Unlike others who merely castigated Wyden, they took a different and more honest approach. They admitted that much of what he wrote was true. Terre Haute was indeed behind the times. The city had stagnated for far too long. New efforts and ideas were needed for the city to progress. HELP was fighting not only the physical conditions of Terre Haute but also decades of corruption, indifference and benign attitudes by the men who ran the city.

Their initial statement of purpose noted, "We are not here to crusade against anyone or any thing." Instead, they zeroed in on what would later be called quality-of-life issues. The group pointed out that the city's infrastructure was pitiful. There was no public swimming pool, the sewage system was antiquated at best and open dumps were scattered throughout the city, breeding vermin and disease. There was a crying need to tear down crumbling structures and build anew. The group's abiding theme was

"Urban Renewal." Ultimately, it would be urban renewal that led to the end of the West End.

The group was in step with the era. Initially, it worked with state and local governments and individuals to start modernizing Terre Haute. Over the preceding decade, many other cities had looked at their crumbling, outdated infrastructure as well. But cities needed help. The federal government was looking at the same things. The Department of Housing and Urban Development was created in 1965. A course was set.

Then the old foe roared again.

On Wednesday, May 12, 1965, nearly a quarter of Indiana State University's ten thousand students marched on downtown Terre Haute. After all, there wasn't much else to do—a blown transformer had blacked out the campus. They were marching, they said, to protests the city's "wrongs." Chief among them, it seems, was the red-light district (though a few coeds shouted that they wanted expanded visiting hours in the women's dorms). They marched peacefully and staged sit-ins in front of stores and restaurants on Wabash Avenue. Eventually, some marched through the West End. When Terre Haute police arrested a few students, all but about two hundred returned to campus. Those who stayed behind moved on to City Hall and blocked traffic on Third Street to protest the arrests.

Back on campus, some gathered in front of the administration building. Two student spokesmen met with John Truitt, the dean of students. The dour-faced administrator, never a champion of individual or group rights, told them to disperse. And he promised that the university would try to get their arrested brethren released.

The protests dominated the next few issues of the campus newspaper, the *Statesman*. (Terre Haute papers were not publishing due to a strike.) Interestingly, an anonymous *Statesman* staff member offered a sort of primer on visiting the local brothels, titled "The Prostitutes and Me: A Student's Testimonial." Though one senses more than a tinge of male bravado in the piece, it is an honest recounting of one person's ongoing visits to some of Terre Haute's houses of ill fame.

"The first thing you learn when you come to Indiana State," he wrote, "is the prostitution in town." On his first night on campus, some obliging upperclassmen took him on a tour of the West End and its delights. The young man immediately plunged into the scene and had his first experience in a Terre Haute brothel. It was another rite of passage for a callow young student.

He described some of his experiences as a guide to other male students. He was often approached by Black girls in the district asking, "You boys like

Front page of the *Indiana Statesman. Special Collections, Cunningham Library, Indiana State University.*

to come in for a while?" A particular house on North Second Street usually had two girls working per "shift." They locked the door behind you. This "Negro house" was ill-lit and dark. The living room had an old sofa and a stuffed chair holding a "colored woman or man." The room also had a rickety table with a record player and an old radio; a Top 40 or a Nashville country radio station blasted from its tinny speaker. The floors were cheap linoleum, and the house had a "unique aroma" about it.

He often had his choice of two "very attractive colored girls." The price was not mentioned until the girl led him down a dark corridor into a small bedroom furnished with an old chest of drawers, a mirror and an old nightstand with a dishpan and a "variety of antiseptics." Perhaps our young swain was unaware that this was very often the case in most

Where the 'girls' are

Aerial view of the West End in 1965 that appeared in the *Indiana Statesman*. Author collection.

brothels. Waiting to name the price was an excellent "marketing tool." Few men will back out of the deal when their heightened senses override their caution or financial sense.

The prices started at five dollars and "ends where your bankroll ends." Another ISU student had a similar encounter two years later.

> *In the summer of 1967, several weeks after I had graduated from high school, I enrolled at ISU to take two classes I wanted to get out of the way before I started the Fall semester. I lived in Cromwell Hall, which was close to the corner of Mulberry and 3rd Street. It was my first day on campus and, since it was a Sunday evening, the dorms did not provide dinner. Those nights students often ate at Burger Chef, located on the west side of 3rd Street near Mulberry. I was on my way to this popular fast-food establishment when I was greeted by a short, nervous Black man just before I reached the corner of Mulberry and 3rd. He wanted to know if I would be interested in "seeing" several "women friends" of his. Before I could answer, he rattled off a comprehensive menu from which I could choose—young, old, white, Black, tall, short, skinny, or heavy (or any combination thereof). I was taken aback. I had heard stories of Terre Haute's "houses of ill-repute" (and crooked politics), but I never thought I would be pulled into that orbit on my very first night at ISU. I turned him down and went on my way. But weeks later I learned of several men in my dorm who DID accept the invitation. I mentioned this to a graduate student who I knew, and his nonchalant response was simply, "welcome to Terre Haute."*

The *Statesman* articles led to a meeting between Mayor Tucker and university administrators. It was agreed that ISU and the City of Terre Haute needed to work together to prevent further problems. Thereafter, the campus police and Terre Haute police met regularly to compare notes about student activities.

Indiana State opened its doors in 1870. It protested prostitution in the city from the beginning. It viewed itself as the guardian of the health and welfare of its young charges. That was made difficult when there were brothels within a short walk on all sides of the campus to tempt male students into sin.

Throughout its evolution from Normal School to university, ISU pressured the city to do something about "this evil." This was especially true during the world wars, as the campus hosted training programs for the military. The idea of the school buying up available plots all around it to form a buffer between it and the houses began early. In 1914, the university began doing just that. It continued over the years. It was the school's version of urban renewal before that became a trend in America.

So, when HELP's efforts led to urban renewal in Terre Haute, the campus administrators eagerly joined the process.

In 1962, the Department of Housing and Urban Development's predecessor, the Urban Renewal Administration, granted Terre Haute almost $6 million for its projects. The city formed the Community Center Urban Renewal Project. The funds were meant for the west central part of the city and areas around Indiana State. Approximately $150,000 of it was given to the university for a planning study.

Indiana senator Vance Hartke announced that the project would concentrate on removing a blighted area (the West End area) of nonresidential buildings west of the campus and four hundred housing units, most of them substandard. When cleared, the land would be used for college expansion and industrial development. Over the next few years, plans were developed to get the machinery rolling. One of the ideas was to build a civic auditorium; the West End was considered a prime site.

First, the buildings and real estate needed to be appraised. Once that was done, property owners were offered what was seen as fair market value. If they refused, the right of eminent domain was invoked, and the owners were forced to sell. And what about those who lost their homes or businesses? In 1966, when the project director was asked about relocating families, he was blunt and unsympathetic. "We have given up the practice of a man's home is his castle. We cannot put one individual or business over the rest of the community." In other words, you are on your own, folks.

Demolition of some of the buildings near ISU began in 1967, with forty-seven structures torn down during the year. The West End's time was coming.

The Renewal Project took out options on two of Meharry's properties, at 210 and 214 Cherry, in January 1968, offering her $27,900 for them. The latter was Meharry's favorite place. She bought it in 1940 and turned it into a brothel to rival any in the West End. It was not losing the brothel business that upset her. She had already opened operations elsewhere. She simply loved the house. It was well built, and she had spent over twenty-five years decorating it. Mcharry tried to make a deal with the project. She would give them the lots free if they let her move 214 to another location. She was told it was too much trouble and that the Chicago Regional HUD office would not allow it.

Mary Moon's house was optioned at the same time, and Nell Bandy's came in April. Soon, roaring machines with huge claws and wrecking balls began nibbling away at the West End.

Cheryl Dean was a young ISU student who took a temporary job with the Terre Haute Area-Planning Department. One of her jobs was to verify measurements of the buildings that were being torn down. She still remembers Madam Brown's house.

I was on assignment to the Circle R Hotel but of course, I knew it to be the brothel of Madam Brown. When we had the assignment, it was run by a couple, I cannot recall if they were the owners at the time. I entered via a back door from a courtyard where the original pool had been but there was no longer a pool, only a large cement fountain. The back entry led through a kitchen on the first floor into the brothel or at that time hotel and I use the term hotel loosely because it still had lose rate interpretation—some referred to as hourly. I was told that after the brothel closed, the facility still rented rooms to gentlemen who brought their lady friends for a rendezvous without being seen.

I briefly glanced around the first floor but was assigned to the second floor where there were bedrooms. As I recall they were large rooms that were clean and well kept, as I recall there were eight or possibly nine rooms and a community bath. I remember one bedroom on the south side of the hallway that had large windows that overlooked the side yard and I believe a fountain. The room had heavy bedroom furniture and a wardrobe with dark wood floor and decorative wood work, as a well as an oriental type rug. I remember because the amount of light from the windows. The back bedrooms on either side of the hallway overlooked the enclosed, I think fenced, back area where there was a multiple car garage. The building was brick and was either yellow brick or painted yellow.

Again, it has been several years, but I recall a south side entrance that had a high counter like a registration desk. I glanced around the first floor because I was interested in seeing Madam Brown's boudoir but of course, by the time I visited it was someone else who was residing in the rooms. As I recall, there were two bathrooms on the first floor one; would have probably been exclusively for the madam along with a bedroom and sitting room or parlor. The bedroom of which I speak, was on the north side of the building. There was a dining room and living room with several chairs and side tables, of course there was a front entry to the hotel. Off the kitchen was an area that the lady said could have been the cook's or housekeeper's quarters at one time.

As a young person, I can still remember thinking it must have been a beautiful facility in its prime because it still had some rich wallpaper, although well worn, and dark ornate woodwork. My impression was that in its day it was probably a magnificent brothel because by the late 60's it still had good bones and a touch of class.

Even before urban renewal, the West End was losing its brothels. Times were changing, and madams grew older and retired from the business. The time of the designated vice district was all but over. Even the legendary Storyville in New Orleans was all but gone. The brothel culture was ending. More and more girls who would have worked West End houses were working for pimps or for themselves, plying their trade in bars and hotels. One such place was the once fashionable Indois Hotel at Third and Wabash Avenue. By the 1960s, it had decayed into a seedy spot frequented by pensioners and girls with their johns. By that point, the Indois was so depressing that it made you feel either sad or unclean just driving by it.

And while all that was going on, Ralph Tucker was succeeded by Leland Larrison in 1968. The new mayor, a Republican, was much different than Tucker. He was a dour, blunt-spoken man. He did share Tucker's view that prostitution was a necessary evil, but he had more important items than brothels on his agenda, such as getting a railway overpass built.

Larrison, of course, was long familiar with madams and brothels from his days making deliveries there from the family drugstore. He said there were only three "known" brothels and eighteen prostitutes when he took office in 1968, all of which could be seen from his office. That was not an accurate observation. Maryann Meharry and three other West End madams sought a meeting with Larrison. They convened in his office soon after the election and asked him what was ahead for them during his administration. His reply heartened them. "All I want you to do is run them houses like it should be done. I don't want no trouble down there. I don't want any criticism on my part. If you run 'em right, I don't think there'll be too much to it. And we'll continue."

They then asked him what percentage of their take he wanted for protection. He bluntly stated that he wanted none. And he didn't want any Christmas "gifts" from them. (He did accept some small things, like an electric cigarette lighter.) The madams left his office breathing easier than they had when they walked in.

Actually, it was Larrison and his chief of police who stirred up controversy about prostitution. A wire service report that one of his campaign promises was to eliminate prostitution and gambling in Terre Haute angered the mayor so much that he went on local television to deny he had ever made such a promise. It seemed an odd thing for a mayor to defend prostitution, but that was Terre Haute. The story caused *Time* magazine to take a closer look at the situation in Terre Haute in its February 21, 1969 issue. "The mayor's firm stand in defense of vice raised a modest cheer from gamblers in the upstairs room at the Club Idaho on Hulman Street, and then they went back to their roulette and poker."

The report also mentioned the large sign on the door that advised, "What you see, what you hear, when you leave, leave it here."

The article recalled the history of Terre Haute's all-encompassing vice. There were some, however, who were utterly shocked by Larrison's stance and his belief that prostitution should be legalized. Chief among them was Allen Rankin, president of Indiana State University. Rankin joined a long line of Indiana State presidents who had lobbied for the closure of the brothels since the 1880s. After all, "Brand new high-rise dormitories [on the ISU campus] now stood across the street from battered old brownstones that housed the brothels."

Larrison snidely said that he would close the brothels "if the college will get rid of the beatniks, kooks and hippies over there." Police Chief Glen Means decided to help out by tossing a filling station's worth of gasoline on the fire. He echoed the truism that prostitution was a necessary evil and that there had not been a single incident of rape reported in the previous year. Not satisfied with that, he went on to utter a sexist denigration of women and rape. "Oh, a few college girls hollered rape, but it really wasn't."

While the hoopla continued, Vigo County sheriff Clyde Lovellette raided three houses in the district and arrested nine women. The county court sentenced them to fifteen days in jail. Larrison worried that the six-foot, nine-

A cheap tabloid called *The Truth* sensationalized Terre Haute. *Vigo County Public Library Archives.*

inch Lovellette, a former All-American basketball player who led Kansas to an NCAA championship in 1952 followed by a long career in the NBA, was merely positioning himself to run against the mayor in the next Republican primary. The article was described by some as another sensational broadside aimed at Terre Haute. Even President Rankin, a critic of Larrison, wrote him a note saying that even though he seldom agreed with him, he thought the article was unfair.

Larrison actually had a chance to close the West End for good but did not take the opportunity. When urban renewal was about to tear down the last of the red-light brothels, three madams, including Maryann Meharry, went to see Larrison. They said they wanted to stay together and continue to operate. They wanted to move a few blocks north on First Street. He agreed, as long as they abided by the previous agreement and caused no trouble. It never happened.

It seemed someone wanted to hasten the destruction of at least one house. Nell Bandy and two of her girls were watching television and waiting for customers one evening in February 1968. It was a quiet evening in the house until an explosion knocked them out of their seats. Someone had placed dynamite on the side of her one-story house at 108 North Second. The blast blew a hole in the wall and unseated Nell and the girls. Windows around the neighborhood were shattered, and debris fell like a black rain on the streets. Bandy was at a loss as to who might try to kill her. Debris was scooped up and sent to the crime lab at the FBI, but nothing came of the investigation. It just made it easier to later tear down the house.

THE GREAT RENEGADE RAID OF 1970

Terre Haute did not have a happy police force in the first months of 1970. On January 22, Mayor Larrison used his state of the city address to castigate his law-enforcement officers. They were simply not doing their job, he said. He was upset that traffic accidents increased 49 percent and fatalities a whopping 67 percent in 1969. He had specifically asked them to pay attention to parking the wrong way on the streets and minor traffic violations. If the violations were minor, they did not have to cite the offenders, just warn them that they were breaking the law and would be punished if it happened again. Obviously, they did not follow his orders. "I did not get cooperation from the majority of the policemen."

The men in blue did not take kindly to being called out by the mayor for not doing their jobs. They were not all that pleased with Police Chief Glen Means or his subordinates, either. Angry conversations reverberated in parking lots, the Fraternal Order of Police lodge and cop bars. What should they do? They could go on a ticket-writing spree, cite everything from jaywalking to double parking. But what good would that do except piss off a few drivers? No, they needed to do something that would really get noticed.

So, on February 5, twenty disgruntled cops decided they would shake things up. They agreed to meet when they were off duty and dressed in plain clothes. They would show Larrison what big-time policing was.

At around 1:00 a.m., Maryann Meharry heard her night maid open the door. When her house at 214 Cherry was demolished, she moved a few blocks north and bought an apartment building and a house next to it at 722 North Fifth. Five guys dressed in white shirts and black slacks entered the house. Maryann kidded them about being dressed alike and asked if there was a convention in town. Just then, one of the men walked

GOING TO COURT—Some of the women arrested in raids on alleged houses of prostitution early Friday morning as they were being taken from the county jail where they spent the night to city court for an appearance Friday morning. Police matron Betty Inglert (left) escorts the women to their court date.

Strausburg Photo.

The Great Raid of 1970. This is the first time that photos of girls appeared in newspapers. *Author collection.*

into the room tightly holding one of her girls, Mae, by the arm. Maryann laughed, "What, are you afraid she'll run away." "No," the man said. "I am a policeman. And you are all under arrest." Maryann had never been arrested before.

They arrested five of her girls and three ISU students. The supreme irony was that the encounter was relatively innocent. Michele, one of Meharry's prettiest girls, had fallen for a college boy. She often brought him to the house after dates on her days off. This time, he brought along two buddies to see what a brothel was like on the inside. They were just sitting around drinking Cokes and waiting for their friend to finish when the cops burst in. They pushed open the bedroom door, and even though Michele and her boyfriend had "finished" and were dressed, they were arrested. It was off to jail for everyone.

While Meharry and her crew were being arrested, policemen were raiding four other houses, including Audrey Dorsey's.

Later that day, the afternoon paper hit the streets with the headline "30 Jailed in Police Raids." The thirty included five madams, fifteen girls and ten men, five of them ISU students. For the first time, there were photos of the girls and madams, who were trying to shield their faces as they were being

Visiting, too young to be a client. *Lawson collection.*

taken into the jail. The renegade policemen were smart enough to give the papers a heads-up about the raids so that photographers could be there to record the scene. Two people not warned about the raids were Mayor Larrison and Police Chief Means. Means was vacationing in Florida. The officers showed them what their police department could do!

To further embarrass Larrison and Means, the twenty renegade policemen issued a disingenuous statement that the action was not a "political" move. It was intended to let people know that "policemen have done our job and now it's up to the prosecutor and judge."

The college boys had their names printed in the paper and were fined fifty dollars plus costs. It probably led to very uncomfortable conversations with college authorities and families. Everyone else was released on bond and would later be fined.

Mayor Brighton "shuts the lid" in 1972. *Author collection.*

All of the raided houses were outside the confines of the West End. Time and urban renewal had done their work. The West End was gone, obliterated from all but memory. It would take another mayor with another idea to shovel the last sprinkling of dirt on the district and those forced to leave it.

William Brighton succeeded Larrison in 1972. He made efforts to clean up Terre Haute's terrible image. Brighton took offence at a Larrison statement aimed at him during the election campaign. Larrison cast doubt that the crusading Brighton could do any better than previous mayors. "Even if Jesus Christ were mayor...we'd still have a bad reputation." Brighton answered that "as long as we have a red light district within two or three blocks from City Hall and adjacent to a growing Indiana State University it's impossible to put our best foot forward." He set about clearing the path ahead for Terre Haute.

Brighton said that ten to twelve brothels employing nearly one hundred prostitutes still remained in the city. He ordered a major change that rang as the death knell of truly organized prostitution in the city.

Previously, being convicted of prostitution meant a fine that was imposed as a sentence. Those arrested might spend a night in jail until they could make bail, but that was usually the extent of their stays. Brighton announced that prostitution would be prosecuted as a felony, with a sentence of from one to five years. Suddenly, madams and prostitutes faced hard jail time if they carried on as before. The mayor then flooded suspect areas with police to enforce the policy. A few weeks later, he turned his attention to gambling. That, too, was closed down—or mostly closed down. Gambling went on quietly for years at several clubs in town, particularly the Idaho Club.

After over a century and a half of rampant prostitution and gambling, Terre Haute was "Sin City" no more.

Conclusion

BACKWARD GLANCES

ndiana State University won its own Hundred Years' War with the West End. Roughly one-third of the West End is now owned by the university. Where brothels once stood are now parking lots, dorms and sports fields. The site of Edith Brown's house is now student apartments. The campus streets once roamed by girls and pimps are filled with skateboarders and joggers.

The only people now living in the West End are those in the student apartments. Maryann Meharry's house is now a Social Security office. Lawyers' offices and fading businesses sit along Second Street. Once the liveliest street in town, to walk down it on a Sunday today is to trod a concrete ghost town.

Today, Terre Haute still has an interesting relationship with the West End. Some do not want to have the history even acknowledged. "Why bring up the past?" is their lament. But many others embrace it as a colorful period and want to know more, to know what is myth and what is truth (hence this book). One still encounters those who will tell you they only know two things about Terre Haute: the West End and Larry Bird.

To its credit, the Vigo County Historical Society has not shied away from telling the story. Edith Brown's Tiffany canopy graces the entrance to one of its rooms, and Brown is part of the permanent exhibit on the history of Terre Haute. Over the years, the society has offered several programs on Brown, including one called "The Madam and the Saint." That very popular program features women portraying Brown and that other famous Vigo Country woman, Saint Mother Theodore Guerin.

Second and Cherry, looking north, 2022. Once the busiest street in the West End, it's now all but deserted. *Author photo*.

Edith Brown display at the Vigo County History Center. *Suzy Quick photo*.

The Last Madam

Maryann Meharry gave up the "madaming" business in 1974. She continued her involvement in multiple community groups, especially those aiding veterans. She and her daughter owned two taverns in Terre Haute for a while. Maryann was tough. She had to be in her business. While other madams had bouncers at their houses, Maryann did not. Her daughter recalled that Maryann was tough even as a child. If other kids tormented her, she literally took care of it with her own hands, knocking her antagonist to the ground. She was known to throw out unwanted guests and packed a punch that could knock a man out of a chair. As with her houses, Maryann brooked no nonsense in the tavern, once defending herself with a knife against an abusive patron. She was always ready to protect herself or others and carried a switchblade and a gun with her into her eighties. At that age, she was fond of showing her grandkids how to use nunchucks.

Ever the businesswoman, she continued to buy and sell houses. Maryann never lost her passion for antiques. Her collection grew to such proportions that she had to store it in several houses around town. She was always happy to share her collection with the public.

She died in 1993 at age ninety-one. The last of the West End madams was gone.

Growing Up in the West End

Maryln Meharry was literally born into the West End. She was adopted by Mickey and Maryann Meharry as a baby. She grew up in the family home next to her mother's brothel at 214 Cherry. It was a very happy childhood. To her, the West End was just like any neighborhood. It was home.

It was the place she felt safe. The once raucous streets of the West End were now quiet. Most of the noise now came from her and her playmates as they rode bikes, played hide-and-seek or hopscotch and generally ran around the neighborhood. She wasn't looked down upon because of her mother's business. She remembers it as a good place where neighbors helped out neighbors in tough times—just like scores of other neighborhoods around Terre Haute. It was only later, as she grew up, that Maryln found that some outside the West End had a much different view of her and her neighborhood.

Maryln Meharry and
the beloved family
housekeeper, Myrtle,
circa 1957. *Lawson
collection.*

It wasn't until she was twelve or thirteen that Maryln figured out exactly what the family business was. Things began to snap into place. Her mother did not talk to her about it or explain her life. Like many American families during this period, kids were shooed away when adults had serious things to discuss. Maryln didn't mind. She would much rather be outside with her friends than sit around listening to adults jabber about things. Only in her later years did Maryann sometimes talk to her daughter about her business and life as a madam.

She, and sometimes her friends, were allowed in the house when no "business" was taking place. She enjoyed being around the girls. They treated her like a kid sister or a little niece. They taught her how to do the jitterbug, colored with her and played games. She often sat on their laps. Later, when Maryln was pregnant, they brought her a closet full of baby clothes. When she lost a child, the girls got together on their own to send beautiful flowers. It was a heartfelt gesture that was much appreciated.

It was outside the West End that Maryln encountered difficulties. She quickly learned than many refuse to look at the individual for who they are. Instead, they craft an identity for a person based on what they have heard or read about them. She went to Sacred Heart, a local Catholic school, through the eighth grade. Classes were small, and everyone knew one another. As she said, "I went to church six days a week." She was accepted.

One of the girls holding
Maryln Meharry, circa
1952. *Lawson collection.*

The shock came when she went to Garfield, a public high school. High school can be difficult for most people, but it was sheer torment for Maryln. She hated it. Her classmates heard the wild tales and myths about the West End. She was no longer Maryln Meharry. She was that girl from the West End, the "Whore."

Rumors spread that she was a prostitute. Maryann Meharry opposed abortion, but when a desperate father came to her asking if she knew of a doctor who would terminate his fourteen-year-old daughter's pregnancy, she reluctantly said she would find out. When word got out about that, rumor spread that it was Maryln who wanted an abortion. Other students called her "whore" and "slut." When words didn't suffice, they knocked out the headlines of her first car and defaced it. They damaged her school locker and left nasty notes on it.

There were times when being a Meharry put Maryln in real danger. When she was thirteen, she was alone at the farmhouse the family moved into after the West End buildings were torn down. A man came to the door and asked her if she wanted to "party." He left only when her older sister came home and scared the man off. That scene would play out at least two more times in her young life. After Maryln married, she was living in a house her mother owned when two similar encounters occurred. Both times, the men wanted to party and had to be fended off. She had no idea how they found her. She was using her married name, but somehow they found out she was connected to the Meharrys and assumed she was carrying on the business.

Thus Maryln learned the hard way that the Meharry name carried connotations for some. But what others think long ago stopped bothering her. Like her mother, she is a straightforward woman of common sense who stands up for herself and her family. She is proud of her parents. They were good people always willing to help out others. If their occupations bothered some people, that was their problem. They lived their lives as best they could. That is one of the reasons she has always been truthful about her parents' lives and where she grew up. She has been very open with her children and grandchildren about the past. She wants them to know the truth, in case outsiders bring it up. She wants them to know that they have nothing to be ashamed of about the family past.

Looking back, Maryln is happy with her life growing up in the West End. She felt safe walking the streets. Every parent looked out for all the kids in the neighborhood. It was a time when people did not have to lock their doors. She would not trade it for any other childhood, parents or neighborhood.

Most of all, she wants others to understand that the people of the West End were just that, people. Their lives and circumstances were different than most, but they were trying to live their lives.

The memory of the West End lives on.

SELECTED SOURCES

Introduction: The Boundaries of Sin

Bergstrom, Laura. "Hautian Houses of Ill-Fame: A Midwestern City's Confrontation with Vice, 1910–1972." Unpublished master's thesis, Indiana State University, 2003.

Kiere, Mara L. *For Business & Pleasure*. Baltimore, MD: Johns Hopkins University Press, 2010.

Saturday Spectator (Terre Haute, IN), November 11, 1922, p. 10.

Terre Haute Common Council minutes, August 6, 1906.

The Golden Age

McCormick, Mike. *Terre Haute: Queen City of the Wabash*. Charleston, SC: Arcadia Publishing, 2005.

Outlook. "The Terre Haute Bribery Case." March 1915.

Rosen, Ruth. *The Lost Sisterhood: Prostitution in America, 1900–1918*. Baltimore, MD: Johns Hopkins University Press, 1982.

Saturday Spectator, July 28, 1917, p. 20.

Saturday Spectator, January 20, 1914, p. 20.

Stimson, Stella. "The Terre Haute Election Trial." *National Municipal Review* (March 1916).

The Yo-Yo Years: The 1918–23

Saturday Spectator, July 28, 1917, p. 20.
Saturday Spectator, October 27, 1917, p. 3.
Saturday Spectator, August 21, 1920, p. 1.

Settling In: The Second Golden Age and Beyond

Anonymous. *Prostitution-Terre Haute*. Vigo County Oral History Project, Special Collections/Archives. Vigo County Public Library.
Crumrin, Timothy. *Wicked Terre Haute*. Charleston, SC: The History Press, 2019.
Lawson, Maryln. Interview with author.
Saturday Spectator, March 30, 1935, p. 15.
Saturday Spectator, September 11, 1937, p. 3.

People of the West End

Maryln Lawson. Interview with author.
McCormick, Mike. *Terre Haute: Queen City of the Wabash*. Charleston, SC: Arcadia Publishing, 2005.
Saturday Spectator, April 1, 1916, p. 5.
Saturday Spectator, May 24, 1930, p. 4.

Madams

Anonymous, *Prostitution-Terre Haute*. Vigo County Oral History Project, Special Collections/Archives. Vigo County Public Library.
Kiere, Mara L. *For Business & Pleasure*. Baltimore, MD: Johns Hopkins University Press, 2010.
Maryln Lawson. Interview with author.

A Girl's Life

Anonymous. *Prostitution—Terre Haute*. Vigo County Oral History Project. Special Collections/Archives. Vigo County Public Library.

Kiere, Mara L. *For Business & Pleasure*. Baltimore, MD: Johns Hopkins University Press, 2010.

Maryln Lawson. Interview with author.

Revival and Decline: 1946–61

Anonymous, *Prostitution–Terre Haute*. Vigo County Oral History Project. Special Collections/Archives. Vigo County Public Library.

Batman, Howard. Vigo County Oral History Project. Special Collections/Archives. Vigo County Public Library.

Bowers, John. *The Colony*. New York: Greenpoint Press, 1973.

Hendrick, George, Helen Howe and Don Sackrider. *James Jones and the Handy Writers' Colony*. Carbondale: Southern Illinois University Press, 2001.

Jones, James. *From Here to Eternity*. Rev. ed. New York: Random House, 2012.

Kadel, Robert, Vigo County Oral History Project, Special Collections/Archives. Vigo County Public Library.

The Lowney Turner Handy Writers' Colony: Marshall, Illinois, 1952–54. Special Collections, Indiana State University, Cunningham Library.

Maryln Lawson. Interview with author

Nasser, Paul. Vigo County Oral History Project, Special Collections. Vigo County Public Library.

Saturday Spectator, August 15, 1925, p. 4.

The Long Goodbye, 1962–72

Bergstrom, Laura. "Hautian Houses of Ill-Fame: A Midwestern City's Confrontation with Vice, 1910–1972." Unpublished master's thesis, Indiana State University, 2003.

Dean, Cheryl. Correspondence with author.

HELP Collection. Vigo County Public Library Archives.

Leland Larrison. Vigo County Oral History Project. Special Collections/ Archives. Vigo County Public Library.

Maryln Lawson. Interview with author.

Spann, Edward. *Ralph Tucker of Terre Haute: A Mayor and His City, 1938–1977.* Terre Haute, IN: self-published, 1998.

Terre Haute (IN) Tribune. "Vice Lid Is On— Brighton." January 12, 1972.

ABOUT THE AUTHOR

Tim Crumrin is an award-winning historian and author. He received the prestigious Eli Lilly Lifetime Achievement in Indiana History Award from the Indiana Historical Society in 2014 for his contributions to history.

His previous works include *A Sky Held Captive*, a collection of short fiction and poetry, and *Til the Coal Train Hauled It Away: A Memoir of the Rise and Decline of a Small Town*. He has written two other books on the history of Terre Haute, *Wicked Terre Haute* and *Hidden History of Terre Haute*.

He lives in Terre Haute with his wife, Robin, and two dogs, Clary and Cadie, who graciously allow him to share their office.